D0095972

Task Groups
in the
Social Services

SAGE SOURCEBOOKS FOR THE HUMAN SERVICES SERIES

Series Editors: ARMAND LAUFFER and CHARLES GARVIN

Recent Volumes in This Series

Task Groups in the Social Services

**Marian Fatout
Steven R. Rose**

Sage Sourcebooks for

the Human Services Series

30

SAGE Publications
International Educational and Professional Publisher
Thousand Oaks   London   New Delhi

HV
41
.F365
1995

Copyright © 1995 by Sage Publications, Inc.

All rights reserved. No part of this book may be reproduced or utilized in any form or by any means, electronic or mechanical, including photocopying, recording, or by any information storage and retrieval system, without permission in writing from the publisher.

For information address:

 SAGE Publications, Inc.
2455 Teller Road
Thousand Oaks, California 91320
E-mail: order@sagepub.com

SAGE Publications Ltd.
6 Bonhill Street
London EC2A 4PU
United Kingdom

SAGE Publications India Pvt. Ltd.
M-32 Market
Greater Kailash I
New Delhi 110 048 India

Printed in the United States of America

Library of Congress Cataloging-in-Publication Data

Fatout, Marian.
    Task groups in the social services / Marian Fatout, Steven R. Rose.
        p.   cm.—(Sage sourcebooks for the human services series;
    v. 30)
    Includes bibliographical reference and index.
    ISBN 0-8039-5449-2 (alk. paper).—ISBN 0-8039-5450-6 (pbk.:
    alk. paper)
    1. Social service.   2. Social work administration.   3. Decision-
    making, Group.   4. Group problem solving.   5. Small groups.
    6. Work groups.   I. Rose, Steven R.   II. Title.   III. Series.
    HV41.F365   1995
    361'.0068'4—dc20   94-46669

This book is printed on acid-free paper.

99   00   01   10   9   8   7   6   5   4   3

CONTENTS

PREFACE

Task groups are tied into many social systems. They influence families, are sites for peer interaction, are present in work settings, are part of community interaction, and provide means for carrying out governmental functioning. Many persons have had experiences in task groups in school and work environments. The functioning of task groups, which allows people to work together to accomplish their goals, is a dynamic process. Many types of social service agencies make use of task groups to fulfill their purposes. Those working in such agencies spend considerable effort at work in various types of task groups including boards, committees, teams, treatment conferences, and social action groups.

Knowledge about the skills of working with task groups has developed over time, as has the organization of such groups. The very earliest of such groups were probably clans and tribes. Much later, during the industrial revolution in America, task groups were used by labor unions, adult education, settlement houses, brotherhoods, and character-building agencies. With the organization of the American Association for the Study of Group Work recognition of common processes and practices that occur in task groups had begun. At that time group work was used in educational, religious, and leisure-time settings.

Over time group work became more closely linked to and later became part of the social work profession. Early leaders of the profession disagreed over the appropriate use of this method. (Even today, some controversy exists about the place of group work in the education of social workers.) A debate raged about whether groups should be used to help people to change, to change the environment, or to produce a product. It took many years for a distinction to be made in the profession between therapeutic and task groups. Many practitioners saw both therapeutic and task purposes occurring simultaneously in groups. It was during this period that for many a clear differentiation was made between therapeutic groups (changing people) and task groups (producing products). Today a distinction is frequently made between groups for therapeutic purposes and those for accomplishing tasks, which is an assumption underlying this book.

As the social work profession evolved, much of the practice and theory development focused on therapeutic groups, with less expansion of theory and practice in task groups. Work with groups is an ever expanding area of practice in the social services. Today many professions are developing and refining knowledge about working in task groups. By integrating some of the concepts and methods used in various settings and by implementing these practices in the delivery of social services, more creative and purposeful services may be provided.

As behavioral scientists have studied and researched the dynamics and functioning of small groups, the knowledge and skills in working with groups have expanded. In order for positive products of task groups to result, knowledgeable guidance must be provided. In social service organizations, this is often the function of the staff members. A guiding objective of this book is to develop material that will be useful to those who are or will become social service professionals who participate in task groups, including those in a position to supervise and educate social service providers who work in task groups.

The focus of this book is on task groups whose purpose includes accomplishing a goal or producing a product such as a plan of action, a budget, or a solution to a problem. The purpose of this book is to bring together current knowledge and skills in the area of task group practice in the social services. The specific intent of this book is to help social work students and social service practitioners develop a sound base of practice in working with task groups.

OVERVIEW OF THE BOOK

The book begins with a description of the historical development of interest in groups in the delivery of social services. Subsequently, a description is provided of the planning and development of task groups for a variety of purposes. The role and functions of the practitioner in working with task groups are described with a dual emphasis on both task and socioemotional behaviors. The book highlights other issues pertaining to task groups, including working with persons with problematic behaviors, using the problem-solving process, using both small group and large group decision-making techniques, and evaluating process and outcomes in groups.

OUTLINE OF THE BOOK

This book consists of 10 chapters. The first chapter serves as an introduction to the historical development of contemporary interest in social service practice with task groups. It highlights the historical period in the United States when practice with groups generally began to be recognized, developed, and later merged with professional issues. This chapter notes issues including disagreements and conflicts concerning the appropriate use of groups and suggests possible resolutions of the various points of view.

Chapter 2 discusses methods of differentiating task groups from other types of groups, such as therapeutic groups, and considers overlapping areas. It also identifies and describes the variety of task groups used in social service practice, including administrative groups, committees, delegate councils, teams, treatment conferences, focus groups, and social action groups. As each type of group is described, emphasis is placed on the purpose, methods for attaining members, sources of rules of procedure to be followed, duration, roles of practitioners, and examples of social service settings and situations in which these task groups exist.

Following the presentation of the various types of task groups, we focus in Chapter 3 on the planning, composing, and recruiting of members. The issue of individual versus group problem solving is discussed. Factors to be considered in planning task groups are explained, including the social context, size, duration, time, frequency, and physical environment. Group composition is an important aspect of planning that includes consideration of group cohesion, member motivation, and the knowledge and skills of the potential members. The focus on group composition is followed by a discussion of recruitment that also takes into consideration many factors.

Chapter 4 focuses on teams, which have characteristics of other task groups and whose functioning reflects the influence of small group processes. Teams have some particularly characteristic attributes such as the need for team building. Although shared with other task groups, some characteristics, such as the importance of the use of rewards and communication, take on particular importance in teams. The developmental stages of teams differ somewhat from those of other small groups in regard to their differentiation and therefore are given special consideration in this chapter. The chapter attends to the purposes, functions, and underlying philosophy of teams. Issues relating to field of practice, especially professionalism, and relationships between professions are considered, particularly in regard to interdisciplinary and multidisciplinary teams.

Chapter 5 examines the responsibilities of practitioners for the functioning of task groups in general. Dynamics of group interactions are related with emphasis on communication, cohesion, control, and culture. Group stages are identified with a description of the worker's task and socioemotional behaviors essential to group development. The chapter identifies and describes other specific structures and functions of task group practitioners, including the use of time, agendas, and group minutes.

Despite careful planning and recruitment, most practitioners find problematic behaviors of individuals, subgroups, and the entire task group that interfere with the functioning of task groups. Individual member problems tend to be considered at the group level of analysis. Agendas are seen as problems of subgroups. Problem areas presented and discussed in Chapter 6 include hidden agendas, social loafing, polarization, groupthink, and other member problematic behaviors. Considerable attention is paid to understanding and managing conflicts. Perennial problems in task groups include social loafing and the balance between individual and group processes, which are also seen in such issues as deindividuation and groupthink phenomena. Deindividuation and groupthink reflect tendencies to extreme actions that should be avoided.

The next three chapters deal with the central processes in task group functioning: methods of problem solving and decision making. The task group typically is concerned with solving many types of problems and making many decisions. Chapter 7 deals with knowledge and skills in understanding and working through the steps in problem solving with the group as a sequential process. A special feature of the chapter is its focus on many of the different types of such problems typically experienced by task groups in social service agencies. Finally, the issue of the effectiveness of problem solving in a task group process is considered.

Chapter 8 describes a variety of specific small group decision-making procedures. Special attention is given to providing a conceptual understanding of decisions as they pertain to task group processes, partly because they are related to and affect decision-making processes in task groups.

Task groups have multiple methods of making decisions, including the use of discussion, the push toward consensus, and the use of voting. Nevertheless, obstacles to decision making (e.g., underlying conflicts) and delays and transfers in actually making decisions exist, too. Also presented are special techniques including the nominal group and Delphi techniques, brainstorming, and social judgment analysis. This chapter concludes by exploring the final part of the decision-making process, that is, what follows the actual making of a decision in a social service agency.

Although much decision making in task groups in the social services occurs in small groups, at times large populations of clients or other audiences need to be addressed for such purposes as needs assessment and program planning. Chapter 9 describes large group decision-making techniques, such as parliamentary procedure, Phillips 66 or buzz groups, Crawford slip writing, ideawriting or brainwriting, and the Delphi technique. Each of the techniques is presented in detail for practice application.

Last, Chapter 10 delineates a variety of methods for understanding and conducting task group evaluations. The chapter explores the functions and purposes of evaluation in social service task groups as well as the various types of task group evaluations. Outcome evaluations for determining the effectiveness of task groups are emphasized, with additional attention being paid to the means to such ends through process evaluations. Furthermore, evaluation can serve a purpose in assessing needs and in conducting composition evaluations, all of which help in actually beginning the task group.

ACKNOWLEDGMENTS

We wish to thank our colleagues for their support of our efforts. We acknowledge the encouragement and support of James Midgley and of Howard Karger and appreciate the assistance of Thea Von Lobell and Paula C. Davis. We are grateful to our graduate students who have expressed enthusiasm about the ideas presented in this book.

We thank our editors at Sage who have been helpful to us in the creation and production of this book, including Jim Nageotte, Marquita Flemming, Diana Axelsen, Gillian Dickens, and Alison Binder.

We appreciate the editorial assistance of Charles Garvin in shaping this work.

We acknowledge those who have provided us with inspiration to work in the area of small groups, including Sheldon D. Rose and Vernon Allen.

As authors who shared equally in the creation of this work, we each take responsibility for its content, which we trust will be useful to all who are involved with task groups in the social services.

Marian Fatout and Steven R. Rose
Louisiana State University

Part I

THE NATURE OF TASK GROUPS
IN THE SOCIAL SERVICES

Chapter 1

THE HISTORY OF TASK GROUPS
IN THE SOCIAL SERVICES

The purpose of this chapter is to explicate the intertwined histories of group work and social work and to set the context for the development of the use of task groups. The general approach is one of examining the democratic process as a means for focusing on and ameliorating social problems in task groups. Links with community organization and even the relationship to social casework will also be examined.

HISTORICAL FOUNDATIONS

The beginnings of task groups stretch back in time to ancient civilizations. Task groups were present in early forms of social organizations such as clans and tribes. "The small group is the oldest and most common of all social organizations. Nations and entire civilizations have come and gone, but the small group has continued throughout recorded history" (Mayadas & Glasser, 1986, p. 3). Today, groups are the building blocks of our society. It is within groups that task accomplishment is determined, planned, and carried out. In fact, conceiving of a task activity encompasses the idea of a group as a means of accomplishment.

Knowledge about and practice of task group work in the Western world have occurred within a historical context. "An appreciation of the evolution of work with this system, which later officially became a part of social work, gives perspective in regard to the potential breadth of client populations and problems for which group work can be utilized" (Fatout, 1992, p. 5).

In the mid-1800s major social changes occurred in the United States, partly because of the industrial revolution. Populations shifted from rural to urban areas, and immigration occurred from Europe, Asia, and Central America to the United States. Concomitant with such changes were problems experienced both individually and collectively. Overcrowding, deteriorating neighborhoods, and unhealthy living conditions became common in urban areas. Labor problems resulting from industrialization, the movement of workers from rural to urban areas, and the influx of persons from other countries led to intergroup problems. Women and children became part of the labor force, creating new needs for training, support, and protection from overzealous employers.

Many single men and women moved away from their families and from the rural lifestyle to which they had been accustomed. Even with long working hours, they were often lonely, finding themselves with many hours of leisure time and few, if any friends, in the city. Furthermore, in this era families were fearful that their children would lose opportunities to experience the good life.

During this transitional social time, groups were created with the objective of ameliorating social problems and improving living conditions. Groups were formed in organizations such as settlement houses, the recreation movement, labor unions, adult education, brotherhoods, and Jewish community centers. Two types of group organizations that focused on children and youth were manifest in so-called character-building programs and camp vacations for children. The character-building programs included the Young Men's Christian Association (YMCA), the Young Women's Christian Association (YWCA), the Boy Scouts, and the Girl Scouts. Also at this time, rehabilitation in camps was conducted to help children who developed many preventable illnesses because of the long hours and 7-day workweek spent in relatively dark, poorly ventilated, and otherwise unhealthy factory settings. It was economical for employers to send children out to breathe fresh air and experience sunshine in camps, so that they would become healthy enough to return to work.

Meanwhile, social service providers, who were busily organizing and conducting activities, paid scant attention to theorizing about the commonalities of the medium they were using. Relatively little professional identification among group workers existed at that time. If they were asked what they did, they tended to respond by indicating that they were Y workers, labor union workers, or recreation workers. There was little awareness among them that they all were using groups to accomplish their varying purposes. Wilson (1976) indicated that they saw themselves working to deal with large social problems "such as poverty, low wages, long working hours, poor housing and exploitation by landlords, inadequate sanitation, political corruption, and caste-class treatment of people" (p. 7). By the 1920s the concept of group was being recognized more broadly as a means of accomplishing a variety of purposes.

EMERGING LINKS BETWEEN
THEORY AND PRACTICE

American society in the 1930s and 1940s provided an atmosphere for the emergence of a new intellectual movement that was an attempt to solve multiple social problems. A major social development influenced the evolution of task groups. Many social and behavioral scientists sought refuge from the horrors of Nazi Europe and came to the United States. They brought to this country a concern with teaching democracy at the grassroots level (Ephross & Vassil, 1988). Many of these scientists had been associated with the universities in Europe and were prepared to begin to apply some of their theories in another society.

One of the theorists identified with social work was Grace Coyle (1930), who attempted to formulate a unified theory of small groups in her doctoral dissertation, *Social Processes in Organized Groups* (published in 1930 as *Social Process in Organized Groups*). The dissertation was based on her many experiences with groups. These experiences included working with women in the YWCA and in industries, conducting discussion groups in the adult education movement, and participating in the settlement house movement with a children's group. To develop her material, she used her working knowledge of small groups and drew on the work of social scientists regarding forms of associations in subgroups, thinking about the community, and the concept of the looking-glass self (Cooley, 1918; MacIver, 1924; Simmel, 1950). Coyle was also associated with John Dewey, Alfred Sheffield, and Mary Parker Follett, who influenced her learning and application of knowledge about task groups.

Dewey (1910, 1966) worked with small group projects and problem-solving groups to teach and demonstrate the concept of learning by doing. His theories were published in his writings *How We Think* and *Democracy and Education*. Dewey was also a member of the first board of trustees at Hull House, one of the original settlement houses in the United States.

Sheffield and Harrison Elliot, along with many other workers, were the prime movers in adult education that resulted in the *Inquiry,* a group of people who created the group workstyle of study and intervention (Siporin, 1986). This association was made up of individuals from settlement houses, adult education, recreation, youth-serving agencies, and groups under religious and secular auspices. After World War I, in response to the social conditions, they hoped to bring about social change, promote democratic communities, and create a better society. Follett (1926) also was concerned about creating positive changes. She organized small groups for enlightened political action and expressed her beliefs in *The New State.* Such associations resulted in the merging of extant knowledge and experience regarding working in task groups. Indeed, it became evident that experience-based generalizations were limited and that systematic investigations were needed in order to further the understanding of groups. From this thinking, group dynamics emerged as a distinct field, and its proponents continued to collaborate with group workers on various research projects.

As noted by Alissi (1980), "Social group work ranks among the earliest practice efforts to realize the potentials inherent in the small group experience to maximize the well being of the individuals and improve social conditions" (p. 6). At the same time, social work has been praised for its philosophical commitments and critiqued for its lack of a scientific base (Lewis, 1991). Practice-based wisdom resulting from experience continued to grow in many organizations, while research attempted to develop deeper understanding of the functioning of task groups. Researchers drew heavily on experiences of Coyle and of Gertrude Wilson and Gladys Ryland at the onset.

With the research and practice that had occurred previously, by the 1930s some common terminology began to develop. Terms such as *purpose, structure, social process, status, roles,* and *stages* of group development had begun to be recognized and used.

A primary underlying theme in the historical development of task groups was the importance of the small group to the functioning of a democracy. Early studies of groups were often focused on leadership, which was related to observations and experiences regarding the emergence and influence of dictators in Germany, Italy, Russia, and Spain. There was a concern for the future of democracy and its leaders. Follett's (1926) work described the group as a key element in the new democratic state. The neighborhood and occupational groups were viewed as democracy's method in opposition to the crowd philosophy (Shapiro, 1991). Lindeman (1921) wrote of "an attempt on the part of people who live in a small compact local group to assume their own responsibilities and to guide their own destinies" (p. 6). It was believed that a democratic state would provide the means for the expression of group differences, which would provide for the common good as they were integrated into the whole.

Basic to the actions of task groups in organizations is the concept of self-help or mutual aid. The terms *self-help* and *mutual aid* also refer to a movement that attempted to deal with some of the same problems as those of the charity organization society, yet differed greatly from it. A major philosophical difference was that the charity organization society viewed poverty as caused by the individual, and group work viewed the cause as social and economical conditions. Typically, the charity organization society did things *to* and *for* people, whereas group work did things *with* people, a difference that created antagonism between the two movements.

PROFESSIONAL DEVELOPMENTS

The group work movement transcended extant fields and professions, and small groups were being used in education, recreation, and religious institutions and settings. As early as the 1920s, Neva Boyd had incorporated group content in recreation leadership courses at Northwestern University and later at Western Reserve University (Boyd, 1971). Classes in group work were taught in 1923 at Western Reserve University. By 1927 a group service curriculum that suggested the beginning of a new approach was established.

One influence on the later merging of group work with social work was the addition of a section for group work to the National Conference of Social Work in 1935. Coyle (1947) and Wilbur Newstetter (1935) presented papers that outlined the philosophy and practice knowledge of group work. By 1936 there were enough belief in and commitment to the use of small groups that the American Association for the Study of Group Work was established. The association promoted study and knowledge building regarding all aspects of work with groups.

Despite questions and concerns about its approach and underlying philosophy, group work continued to grow, schools offered more courses on group work, and agencies were increasingly including group work programs in their overall delivery of social services. By 1946 the study of group work was complete, and the members of American Association for the Study of Group Work took a firm stance, affirming that there was common knowledge and theory about working with small groups. This juncture resulted in the establishment of a new organization, the American Association of Group Workers, which provided a forum for the bringing together of ideas about working with groups from a wide variety of settings. Its publication, *The Group,* disseminated a broad array of thoughts, ideas, and experiences about working with groups.

Early in the development of group work, the focus had been on working with people who had one or more of the following needs and characteristics: being in transition, being disadvantaged, needing to learn new skills or acquire more education, lacking sufficient leisure activities, and needing advocacy and environmental intervention. Gradually, hospitals, family agencies, correctional agencies, and schools began to make use of group work methods. After World War II many veterans returned in need of care, resulting in gains in the number of professional workers and further stabilizing the advances already made in the use of groups.

A major factor that influenced the subsequent merging of group work with social work was the Depression of 1929. During this time group work and casework received funding from the same sources. Group work and casework were also generally dealing with the same type of problems and very similar client populations.

After the National Conference of Social Work in 1935 and the presentation of the group work papers, another major paper was presented to this national conference in 1946. This paper, by Grace Coyle, is considered a milestone in the development of the profession. In it, Coyle concluded that the group work method is within the social work method (Trecker, 1955). There was debate about this matter, especially between group workers, at least until 1955, when the National Association of Social Workers was organized. This organization clearly established and included group work as a method of social work.

EARLY DEVELOPMENTS
WITHIN GROUP WORK

Early group work had been used to help people to change, to change the environment, or to produce a product. Certainly the years immediately following the Depression were focused on environmental concerns. More attention began to be paid to differentiating the type of purpose of group work. Coyle (1959) noted that as early as 1935 and thereafter, there was disagreement about whether group work should move away from its educational and preventive purposes and pursue therapeutic and corrective goals.

During World War II there was special concern and interest in the democratic philosophy. Alissi (1980) wrote of the period following the war that "increasingly, attention was being given to the use of group work for therapeutic purposes, working with formed nonvoluntary groups, developing interracial and intercultural programs, and working on professional issues related to identification, knowledge building, and improving the quality of practice" (p. 19).

Some social and behavioral scientists noted that valid and reliable theory concerning groups during the 1940s was very sparse. However, many studies that would lead to more theory development were underway. During the 1940s and 1950s sociologists and psychologists became very interested in the small group as a unit of study and in knowledge building regarding this phenomenon.

Some researchers focused on the influence of the small group on the behavior of the members in the community and on larger society. Warner, Meeker, and Eells (1949) discovered that "the small group aspects of the family and the clique determined a person's values, class position, life style, and even facilitated his mobility" (Hartford, 1972, p. 18). This study led to hypotheses regarding some factors in the small group that influenced the connections that the individual made with the wider society. At about this same time Samuel Stouffer (1949) was studying the effect of ideology and motivation on the combat record of the American soldier. His findings further demonstrated that it was the small system or group of people that provided the incentive for survival and for improving the individual's functioning in combat.

Other research continued to demonstrate the importance of small group influence on the thinking and behavior of its members. The Roethlisberger and Dickson (1939) studies of Western Electric and Lazarsfeld, Berelson, and Gaudet's (1944) study of voting, *The People's Choice,* were two of the best known works demonstrating this major influence. They were followed by a plethora of studies of small group behaviors and phenomena. In reviewing this period of small group study, Golembiewski (1962) described it as "the most marked research trend in the post World War II social science revolution" (p. 17).

Later, some very significant theories or systems for understanding the functioning of small groups were introduced. George Homans (1950) developed a theory of groups based on an analysis of five types of groups in his book, *The Human Group,* which provides a means for understanding and making use of groups. Kurt Lewin (1935) and the field of group dynamics as identified by Cartwright and Zander (1960) produced another framework for viewing groups and their functioning. Some of the concepts used in this work were composition, cohesion, power and influence, structure, and motivation. Robert Bales (1952) contributed to the theory building by carrying out studies demonstrating that in groups engaged in problem solving, work on the task and work to maintain the functioning of the group occur simultaneously. He identified these member behaviors as instrumental or task behaviors and social-emotional or maintenance behaviors, respectively. Another significant contribution was made by A. Paul Hare, Edgar Borgatta, and Bales (1955), who developed another framework for viewing groups consisting of communication networks, equilibrium, sub-groups, role differentiations, and group size and composition. Many other frameworks for understanding group functioning were developed and continue to be presented today. Because no one set of group concepts seems to be sufficient to explain the very complex functioning of small groups, most group workers draw from a wide variety of conceptions to gain a perception of task group phenomena that is as broad and inclusive as possible.

As these studies were being conducted and reported on by social and behavioral scientists, a number of volumes concerning practice were written by group workers who continued to gain experience in applying their knowledge. Coyle (1947) wrote *Group Experience and Democratic Values,* which emphasized the use of small groups within a democratic framework. A continuation of this perspective was reflected in her book *Group Work With American Youth* (1948). Harleigh Trecker (1948) wrote one of the first textbooks, *Social Group Work: Principles and Practice.* This book continued to be broadly used and was updated and revised twice. A major textbook, titled *Social Group Work Practice* (1949), was written by Gertrude Wilson and Gladys Ryland, two group workers who merged their differing experiences in working with groups and produced a work that was exceptionally inclusive. It described the principles of group work, analyzed program content, and dealt with administration and supervision as processes. By 1951, a book by Helen U. Phillips, *Essentials of Social Group Work Skill* (1951), had been published. It focused on the worker's skill as a primary means for fulfilling social values and purposes. As group work became identified as a part of social work in 1955, it was important that this segment of the profession be able to identify their concerns and means of practice. In 1959, as a part of the Council on Social Work Education's curriculum study, Marjorie Murphy compiled the extant thinking about group work.

DIFFERENTIATION
WITHIN GROUP WORK

As this synthesis and expansion occurred in this developing profession and as leading social work theorists joined with caseworkers in social work, some of the early leaders who had been identified with group work turned elsewhere to meet some of their professional needs (Wilson, 1976). Some group workers who were interested in planning and social action became involved in the newly formed American Association for the Study of Community Organization. This resulted in some division of common effort in understanding and experience in working with groups.

Group work changed as it became a part of social work. "As group work theorists increasingly studied and applied materials from the social sciences they tended to distance themselves from political theory" (Shapiro, 1991, p. 12). At the same time, caseworkers were relying on psychoanalytic theory, which had come into vogue. Group workers were increasingly exposed to these ideas and began to incorporate many of the concepts into their practice. "Until the early 1960s, group work in social work contained an emphasis on contributing to the building of society and a corollary emphasis on the importance of democratic group participation; group workers were to learn skills in working with citizens' groups, in particular" (Ephross & Vassil, 1988, p. 7). From 1960 until about 1975, this emphasis was neglected (Ephross & Vassil, 1993). The focus of social work with groups was on skills in group methods for treatment purposes.

In 1962, the Council on Social Work Education gave formal recognition to community organization as a method of social work comparable to casework and group work (Garvin & Cox, 1987). Despite such recognition, most schools of social work lagged in providing special courses in community organization. Two factors that contributed to this situation were a lack of resources to teach this material and a lack of awareness on the part of potential students. Often, as a part of their learning experience, those relatively few students interested in community organization were placed in classes with group workers, many of whom were interested in therapeutic groups. Certainly, much knowledge is applicable to working with all types of groups, including those whose purpose is treatment, community change, or tasks. Nevertheless, opportunities were often limited for those who were trying to develop their knowledge and skills about community organization and task groups. In some ways, this attempt to teach about small groups used for a variety of purposes in the same classes seemed to contribute to a greater sense of separation between the students who, instead of focusing on their similarities, became more aware of their differing perspectives.

Between 1959 and 1963 the National Group Work Practice Committee of the National Association of Social Workers developed a frame of reference for social group work that listed five purposes of groups: correction, prevention, facilitating normal social growth, personal enhancement, and citizenship responsibility and participation. Across the United States much discussion and disagreement ensued in regard to the appropriate purposes of group work. Agreement was reached that the time had come to drop the purposes of social growth, personal enhancement, and citizen participation. Group work was attempting to focus on so many goals that eliminating these three areas would help to focus the perspective, and in so doing, more emphasis could be given to the corrective and therapeutic goals. This seemed to be timely in that group workers were attempting to enhance their status in the social work profession of the time, in which caseworkers were using psychoanalytic theory to work with their clients.

A lessening of attention to and interest in social enhancement and citizen participation occurred. Many group workers currently interested in task groups regret this movement away from such purposes within this area of practice. Ephross and Vassil (1988) noted that group work had emphasized democratic group participation and contributing to the development of society as primary purposes of groups until 1960. This focus was neglected during the next 15 years.

During this period, group work departed from its traditional purposes, concept, and methods. Pernell (1986, p. 14) has identified concepts that were traditionally used in group work and has contrasted these with those of casework. Several of the concepts that have special significance for understanding the history of task groups are:

Group worker	Caseworker
"member"	"client"
"doing with"	"doing for"
"doing"	"talking about doing"
"mutual aid with the help of the worker"	"worker alone as the agent"
"health and strength"	"sickness and breakdown"

The key words for group work had been *democracy* and *responsible citizenship*.

RECENT HISTORICAL CONTEXT

It is ironic that during a period that deemphasized task groups per se, the War on Poverty—which *relied* on task groups—began. In 1964 President Lyndon Johnson launched this new social program in a campaign that required community organizers. Specific programs established during this time included Head Start, Volunteers in Service to America (VISTA), Job Corps, Neighborhood Youth Corps, Community Action Programs, and many others. Such programs were organized in neighborhoods and communities across the country and required people trained to work as organizers. During this time, group workers interested in working with task groups further distinguished and separated themselves from group workers in agencies working with corrective and therapeutic purposes. Because of the demand for community organizers, salaries for these positions generally exceeded those of agency group workers, resulting at least temporarily in an increased status for community organizers and their field of practice. The War on Poverty also resulted in a closer identification of community organization with the areas of planning and administration (Rothman, 1979).

Accompanying the change in focus of group work was a debate within the profession about the issue of the unity versus the partition of group work. Gisela Konopka (1963) suggested that there were clearly two divisions of group work, one that used groups for individual therapeutic purposes, and another that placed more emphasis on social action. Those who did not believe that it was appropriate to divide group work in this manner included Alan Klein (1970), who asserted that social action is important to ego development and that participation in groups for whatever purpose has the potential for teaching members to participate in democratic social change. The debate about the inclusiveness of purposes in group work has continued to the present time, and differing segments of the profession have functioned from differing perspectives. During much of this time there seemed to be an understanding and at least tacit acceptance of the others' views on this matter. In the literature produced during this time, both views of this situation are included. From time to time there was a reassertion of a strong point of view from one side or the other, but such statements did not significantly change the views of the parties to the debate. With respect to the 1960s, Shapiro (1991) wrote, "This was not a climate that tended to incorporate or reincorporate political theory into group work" (p. 15).

A journal of group work in the social work profession, first published in 1978, bears the title *Social Work With Groups: A Journal of Community and Clinical Practice,* suggesting that the view of group work that recognized specialization of purpose predominated. Furthermore, in the late 1970s and 1980s there was widespread recognition of the economic deprivation and differential opportunities in the United States and in other societies. Racial unrest, experiences of alienation, and conflicts in values were expressed publicly and privately. Also, many group workers became interested in finding ways to institute social change. More recently, group workers have coalesced and merged their perspectives about purposes through the use of terms such as *empowerment* and *advocacy.* The following more integrated view was presented in a paper by Lewis (1989):

> We are reaching for a philosophy base which will bring greater integration of practice—a more holistic approach which makes possible both personal development and attention to the development of humane societal conditions within one practice . . . not as a separate off-shoot more closely identified with community organization, but as an integral part of social group work practice in all of its sites. (p. 27)

It is this attitude that seems to permeate most of the literature and discussion of group workers today.

In writing of the development of group work, Pernell (1986) stated, "It was the particular genius of social group work to bring together into one concept, into one group, and sometimes into one action the concerns for the individual, concerns for the group, and concern for society, and to do this through activities that range from play to social action" (p. 20). This type of model was evident in the beginning development of this approach. This focus was disseminated and changed for some as the National Association of Social Workers was formed and group workers joined caseworkers. The influence of caseworkers using a psychoanalytic perspective led to part of the separation and differentiation within the field. Other major factors contributing to this focus on differential purposes were the specific historical, social, and economic conditions of the Depression and its aftermath; World War II; and the ensuing need for services to soldiers and their families.

Contemporary social conditions are often met with calls for oppressed people to be empowered to change their limiting circumstances and conditions. It is argued that it is the group worker who is most knowledgeable and able to help this happen because many of those working with groups are moving in this direction and gaining experience in this area of service. Further development, differentiation, and integration of specialized knowledge is needed to develop a model for practice that is broad and inclusive enough to enable the practitioner to select the knowledge and methods most appropriate for use with a group whose primary purpose is task accomplishment.

> The group is a bridging concept in social work between our business with individuals and our business with communities. It has content and values distinctly its own, applicable and different emphases to the various purposes and tasks of social work, and important enough to have its unique context preserved and developed for continued enrichment of professional practice as a whole. (Pernell, 1986, pp. 20-21)

CONCLUSION

In this chapter, the development of task groups is understood within the overall perspective of the development of group work. Consequently, this chapter has included an examination of the historical trends that have influenced the development of group work in general and task groups in particular. Some of the major social changes and conditions and the ensuing experiences of populations that called for the use of task groups in organizations as part of the development of social services were analyzed. This chapter provided a review of group work theory, selected intellectual developments, and historical events. Of particular concern were the developments and struggles around democracy that provided much of the social focus of the development of group work. We have also addressed economic changes and developments of the social work profession that provide a perspective for the development of task groups. Among the many changes that were noted was in group work; one issue examined here was that of the unity versus the specialization of method in regard to the purposes of the group. Links between task accomplishment and community organization were explicated.

We now move from history to the contemporary scene. Administrators and staff members in the social services spend considerable time working in task groups, including administrative boards, executive boards, councils, and community action groups, and attending staff meetings, planning meetings, and budget sessions. The following chapter addresses the types of task groups that are used in the social services.

Chapter 2

THE VARIETY OF
TASK GROUPS UTILIZED

As was true in the past, task groups or work groups continue to play an essential role in the organization, planning, and delivery of social services. In regard to terminology, *task groups* has been a label often used to describe the purpose of these groups, and *work groups* is a designation sometimes used to attempt to clarify the distinctive characteristics of these groups. This chapter presents the issue of the dual nature of task and emotion in groups and considers the varied types of task groups used in social service settings.

TASK AND MAINTENANCE IN GROUPS

Task Groups in Relation to Treatment Groups

As indicated in the first chapter on historical development, small groups have always been used to bring about changes in the members or in the group as a whole, to accomplish a purpose, or to produce a product. Attempts have been made to differentiate between treatment (people-changing) groups and groups whose purpose is to produce changes outside the group. Ephross and Vassil (1988) differentiated between the two types of groups by stating that working groups "are those that do not aim at changing the attitudes or behavior of their members, but rather form in order to accomplish some purpose, produce a product such as a plan or budget, develop policies, or participate in a decision-making process" (p. 1). The major difference is that the purpose of the task group is to focus on accomplishing a specific task or on bringing about change outside the group, whereas the purpose of the treatment group is to change the characteristics of people within the group.

This distinction between the two types of groups is a relative one. Although most groups are clearly focused on one purpose, in some instances a task group may become a treatment group or vice versa. An example of a dual purpose group is that of a group of senior citizens who lived in a rural area without bus services. The practitioner recognized that these potential members were very isolated by both their geographic location and the natural processes of aging. Their needs included finding roles, seeing themselves as useful, and interacting with others. As they came together they decided that their primary need was to obtain bus services in the outlying areas of the town. In this instance the group worked at attaining the major goals of both types of groups. Obtaining the bus service became the task, while the interaction, purposeful roles, and affective ties helped to accomplish some therapeutic goals.

Another instance of a group's shifting purposes is that of a small class in a graduate social work program in a university. A group of students were specializing in social work with groups. The professor assigned them a final exam that was to be done as a group project. The assignment was made at the beginning of the semester and the students went to work on the task immediately. Because of their background in treatment groups, they immediately took a treatment group approach. They wanted to really know each other, to take everyone into account, to include everyone's opinion, and to meet each member's psychosocial needs. They continued to work in this manner until about 2 weeks before the exam was due to be returned. Suddenly, the quality of the product took on major importance for each person. In order to produce the very best product that they could, the purpose of the group shifted to that of a task group. Considerably more attention was placed on the product itself with less attention given to social-emotional concerns. As the group handed the exam to the professor, they indicated that for the first time they truly understood the differences between task groups and treatment groups.

It is important to distinguish between these two types of groups because a clarity of purpose helps the entire group, including the leader(s) and the members, to determine the specific area of focus. "In task-oriented groups, the fact that participants are there to work toward some defined tasks that are achieved outside the group means that somewhat less emphasis is placed on the socio-emotional dynamics of the experience" (Northen, 1988, p. 318). In general, the focus is directed primarily to the task to be accomplished rather than to individuals and the entire group.

Task and Social-Emotional Interaction

A distinction has been made in the literature between task and social-emotional (or maintenance) behaviors (Bales & Slater, 1955; Benne & Sheats, 1948). Task behaviors are those acts intended to move the group toward task accomplishment; maintenance behaviors are intended to preserve the group. A typical task behavior is requesting information and summarizing. Commonly used social-emotional behaviors include asking members how they are feeling and asking members why they pick on another member. All members use a variety of both types of behaviors. Research on task groups has revealed that the number of task-focused member behaviors is larger than the number of maintenance behaviors; conversely, in therapeutic groups the greatest number of behaviors are social-emotional in focus, with few task-focused behaviors (Bales, 1955; Munzer & Greenwald, 1957).

With an emphasis on task, more formal structures tend to appear, which can sometimes lead to a reduction in spontaneity, a limitation of member participation, and a dilution of the relationships within the group between the members and with the leader. The members attain their roles in the group by being elected or appointed or by volunteering. The total group network in task groups tends to be more formal than in therapeutic groups. There is an expectation that more formal channels of communication will be used in relation to speaking, conducting business, and recording decisions. Members may raise their hands to be recognized, use Robert's (1989) *Rules of Order* for making decisions, and carefully record the happenings in the meeting. As noted by Northen (1988), "In general, when a group has a very formal structure and clearly differentiated official roles for its members, each person's needs and attitudes will be less apparent than in more informal groups; they are masked by formal procedures" (p. 136).

TYPES OF TASK GROUPS

For relatively inexperienced and unprepared staff members, beginning work in a social service agency can have confusing and baffling aspects. New staff may become aware of an array of small groups, the names of which may not connote the content and method of work being conducted. Groups that are in fact treatment conferences may be called committees. Other terminology, such as *task force*, may be used. The first step in becoming oriented is to determine the purpose of the group. Often the statement of purpose suggests some of the characteristics that one might expect to be operating in that group. The first level of understanding is identifying whether the specific group has a focus of (a) helping members to change or (b) producing a product or bringing about some change outside the group. In general, this answer helps to determine if this is a task group or a therapeutic group.

Task groups are usually categorized as having one of two types of broad purposes. One is serving organizational needs; the other is serving client needs (Toseland & Rivas, 1994). The statement of group purpose helps to identify which of these two areas of service is the primary area of concentration and will be used as a basis for the description of task groups in this chapter. Toseland and Rivas (1994) identify committees, administrative groups, and delegate councils as meeting organizational needs, while teams, treatment conferences, and social action groups meet member needs. An example of an exception to this typology is a group identified as a committee yet really focused on client needs.

A common practice in working with teams, treatment conferences, and social action groups is to appoint subgroups for specific purposes. These smaller units are almost always referred to as committees. Their purpose is either to help with administrative functions of that agency-serving group or to function as a further extension of the client-serving aspect. An example is a subgroup of a group focused on an administrative task, in which the subgroup members compose a mailing list for the larger committee. In contrast, a client-serving committee subgroup might take responsibility for petitioning a social service agency for services on behalf of a segment of the population not being adequately served.

Focus Groups

A type of small group that has received renewed attention, the focus group, is identified and described in recent literature as one that is utilized with both treatment and task groups. According to some authors (Boyd, Westfall, & Stasch, 1981; Smith, 1972; Wells, 1974), focus groups were initially used in market research, although others suggest that the focus group is a fairly general technique that could easily be derived from other sources (Morgan & Spanish, 1984). Focus groups generally bring together participants to discuss a topic of interest to themselves and to the leaders. Focus groups tend to be limited in time to 2-hour sessions.

In marketing research Calder (1977) has identified three types of focus groups, namely, exploratory, clinical, and phenomenological, which are categorized according to their primary purpose. Exploratory focus groups are used to generate hypotheses, clinical groups are expected to provide insights into the participants' unconscious motivation, and phenomenological groups allow the facilitator to observe and understand the participants' commonsense views and everyday explanations.

Focus groups have the potential to be used in a variety of ways in social services. Morgan and Spanish (1984) wrote of the use of focus groups for research purposes, and McKay and Paleg (1992) edited a book describing related uses in psychotherapy. Focus groups also can aid in the discovery of training needs of social service personnel and can be used generally as part or all of the problem-solving process.

Flexibility is a primary characteristic of the use of focus groups. Fern (1982) compared focus groups in regard to factors such as group size, moderated versus unmoderated interaction, and composition of strangers versus acquaintances. Fern found that the number of ideas did not double as the group size was doubled and that the ideas produced in the group were not necessarily superior to those derived from individual interviews. Other findings were that moderated focus groups had some advantages over unmoderated groups and that groups of strangers were preferable to groups of acquaintances.

In focus group process, "interaction can involve activities which do not exist at the individual level such as attempts to resolve incompatibilities, or create shared models. Participants frequently spend the final portions of time in our groups discussing very broad issues, and trying to gauge the amount of consensus on these issues" (Morgan & Spanish, 1984, p. 262). This description of process is in accordance with that of most task-oriented groups. Further development of focus groups for task accomplishment will depend on the creativity and research skills that are utilized.

Administrative Groups

The backbone of a service agency is its administrative groups. "It is the primary function of administration to provide leadership of a continuously helpful kind so that all persons engaged in the manifold workings of the agency may advance the agency to ever more significant service and accomplishment" (Trecker, 1980, p. 335). A board of directors or executive board determines the purpose, goals, and programs for the entire agency. In general, a board is composed of members who are representative of and influential in the community served. The board's legal responsibility and its method of group functioning are based on the articles of incorporation that were developed to create it. The board makes the final determination in all matters regarding services, including the hiring and retention of the executive director. The director's (staff member's) role in this type of administrative group is usually that of facilitating the group by supporting the board president and the group as a whole.

The board provides a structure for communication to and from the agency's subsystems, so that decisions made by this body can reach the other parts of the organization and so that these other units can communicate their views and recommendations to the board. Membership and term of office on the board are determined by appointment or election based on the charter and bylaws of that organization. These administrative systems operate at many different levels within the administrative structure. Examples of this type of organization are seen in many private agencies such as YWCAs and YMCAs, settlement houses, community centers, and other specialized settings.

Another common type of policy- and decision-making board is composed of supervisors, department heads, or other administrative staff. Often in these groups the top administrator assumes the leadership for this group as it makes policy and program decisions. An example of this type of task group is a group of administrators in a county office of human development meeting to determine how to implement a new policy regarding the delivery of social services to the clients. Another example is a nursing unit in a hospital setting that meets on a regular basis to determine policy and practice for administering nursing services within the directives of the top administrative board.

When there are several differing services within the same agency, administrative units usually determine specific program content and policy within that unit. For example, in a settlement house or community center there are usually program committees such as the Committee for Young Adults Program, the Committee for Younger Girls Program, or the Mothers Program Committee. These types of groups are subadministrative systems within the total structure; their policy and practice decisions are subject to review and revision at a higher level by the administrative board.

Committees

Committees are a very common type of task group that all staff in social agencies experience. Committees are also social systems; some may extend over a long time period, while others, such as ad hoc committees, are short term. The outcome of committees is expected to be a product—such as a report, project, or task accomplished—that is the very best possible.

Members are appointed or elected and often serve until the task that is the focus of the committee is accomplished. In selecting a committee, often the organizer looks for variety in knowledge, skills, social networks, and resources in a combination of persons composing the group.

For some planning committees the most important characteristic of members may be that they serve as representatives for particular agency units. For instance, a community center had a 15-passenger bus shared by the center's program units, which regularly competed for use of the vehicle. Until recently the executive director of the center made the decisions about using the vehicle and did the scheduling. To help resolve the conflicts between the units a committee composed of members from each of the program units was appointed. Consequently, the needs and desires of the units were expressed and taken into consideration in planning. The members representing the units reported directly back to their peers about the decisions and how they were made.

Many committees are assigned very complex problems to be resolved. In order to operate more efficiently, the large task is often divided, and a smaller subcommittee is assigned a segment of the total work to be done. On completion of the assignment, the product is submitted to the larger committee.

Most committees use an agenda to give direction to their sessions and encourage a focus on moving toward the desired final outcome. Communication is generally directed to the task at hand. Committees often use Robert's (1989) *Rules of Order* to move through the requisite decision-making process.

Delegate Councils

Delegate councils are task groups composed of delegates or representatives of many smaller units, with delegates usually appointed or elected by the unit that they represent. Usually delegate councils conduct business related to decision making and communications between the larger organization and the smaller units. A great number of delegates meeting together is called a *delegate assembly*. For example, a national organization such as the YWCA calls a delegate assembly of Y-Teen groups from all over the United States. The number of delegates for each state or region is identified, and the local units appoint or elect the persons to attend. If a vital issue is to be discussed at the delegate assembly, local units tend to instruct their delegates how to vote. Each delegate is expected to represent the interests, views, and positions of his or her specific unit.

In some social service agencies, delegate councils are held on a regular basis. For example, a community center that sponsors many adolescent groups may hold a monthly meeting of representatives of each teenage club in order to plan a program for the entire adolescent membership.

Agendas and methods of conducting the meetings of delegate councils are the same as those used in other larger task groups, and, again, decision-making processes and Robert's (1989) *Rules of Order* are commonly used. Votes are taken by units. The delegates keep in constant contact with their constituents in order to truly represent their desires.

Teams

A *team* is defined as "a number of persons associated together in work or activity" (*Webster's Tenth New Collegiate Dictionary,* 1992, p. 1209). (See Chapter 4 for an extensive consideration of teams.) Teams are task groups that are composed of staff members who share one or more concerns having the direct or indirect purpose of serving the client. Examples include professionals who provide treatment for a unit in a residential setting such as a facility for developmentally disabled persons or a psychiatric hospital, a discharge planning team for elderly patients in a medical hospital, and the staff of a settlement house or community center teenage program focused on members with special behavior problems.

The team is a unique type of task group because it is centered on the team members' functioning together in the best possible manner to meet the needs of a client or unit of clients.

> Thus the purpose of coming together as a team is not to "win" one's way or prove one's "rightness" but to utilize the different capacities brought by the different members of the team in order to expand our knowledge and our range of skills so that we can offer the client the best service in the direction that the client wishes to go. (Compton & Galaway, 1984, p. 523)

Often the team is composed of professionals from a variety of disciplines. Because teams must work together to provide the services that are of maximum benefit for the client, it is important that they progress to a later stage of group development. It is expected that this will result in a focus on client needs rather than on interaction among groups. In this type of task

group, more attention is usually given to social-emotional (group maintenance) behaviors than in other types of work groups.

The team often begins with members from a variety of disciplines who may
not know, understand, or appreciate the skills and abilities of the other
professionals. As noted by Kane (1990): "Too often, interprofessional teams
are battlegrounds for rivalrous factions, struggling for power, speaking separate languages, or perhaps not speaking at all to teammates of other professions" (p. 277). As a result, team building must occur over time. So as the team
plans and acts to meet the needs of the clients, the members are also attempting
to learn to know, understand, trust, and cooperate with each other as a group.

The leader of the team may either be appointed by the administrator of
the organization or be elected by the other team members. Often the
appointed leader is a member of the profession that ultimately is held
accountable for the functioning of services on a particular unit. For instance, in a hospital setting for developmentally disabled persons, physicians may be administrators in charge of each residential unit. Often they
are then automatically considered to be the leaders for the team serving
that living group.

Treatment Conferences

Treatment conferences, sometimes called *case conferences,* are composed of professionals who are or soon will be working with a common
client or client system. However, Toseland, Ivanoff, and Rose (1987)
reported that in addition to staff and consultants, on occasion clients,
family, or friends are also included in treatment conference meetings. An
example of a treatment conference is a group of professionals from child
welfare, the school, the mental health department, the probation office, and
a private agency working with juvenile delinquents in a small community
who come together to develop an integrated treatment approach to work
with a young adolescent who is in trouble. Another example is in a hospital
setting in which nurses, social workers, physical rehabilitation workers,
physicians, and staff members from a living facility for elderly are making
plans for the discharge of a client.

The composition of the task group usually changes depending on the
particular case to be discussed. The emphasis in these groups includes
sharing information and understanding about particular situations, decision
making, planning, and implementation. This focus on implementation
usually involves an agreement regarding which member(s) of the group
will carry out the decisions reached in regard to the client.

Ordinarily the particular task group meets only once or at most a very few times. The treatment conference meetings may be called by any of the professionals, often by one who is carrying a primary responsibility for the person or family of concern.

In other instances a treatment conference coordinator takes the responsibility of contacting appropriate persons who have common interest in a particular client system. The coordinator position may result from an administrative appointment within an agency or may develop as a result of the organization of professionals from many agencies within a community, in which case the coordinator is often elected by the other members. A consistent time and place is usually set for these sessions to be held.

Participation in treatment conferences may vary, with either very regular participation by the same members or irregular participation by diverse members. Those treatment conferences focused on a specific type of practice, such as mental health or planning for discharge of patients from the hospital, may have very regular attendance as the client of concern changes. Other groups of this type may meet only on the basis of the client system to be discussed.

Social Action Groups

The purpose of social action groups is to engage in a planned change effort to alter some aspect of the physical or social environment. The focus of concern usually impinges directly on the group members who are affected by the results of their work or on those outside the group who are directly affected by the changes made.

Examples of social action groups include representatives of social service agencies and residents of a housing development working together to develop a plan to reduce the level of drugs, violence, and crime in their area; a group of parents and practitioners developing a plan of action to establish a park in the community; neighborhood residents and staff attempting to get streets and sidewalks paved; and a group of practitioners attempting to obtain funding for a much needed resource in the community.

The role of the practitioner in a social action group tends to vary greatly depending on the purpose and circumstances of formation of the specific group. At times the group or its nucleus is already in existence when the members decide to pursue a specific additional task. For example, the members of a housing project parents group decided to assume the task of cleaning up the surrounding environment. Because there were already officers and other organizational structures within the group, the staff member involved with this social action group functioned as a facilitator and resource rather than taking on a direct leadership role. However, in other instances, such as the practitioner's making efforts to gain additional funding for social services, the social action group was formed to aid in accomplishing this particular task, and staff carried out leadership roles.

In some instances the practitioner and community residents share similar goals. For example, in one neighborhood the residents wished to establish a recreation facility, such as a park for their children, and the practitioner needed outdoor meeting space for adolescents in that same geographical area. By joining forces they worked together to obtain the necessary resources. Nevertheless, the staff member must use caution because the social group has the potential to move in a direction that negates the possibility for its goal to be met, in which case the staff member then determines whether to continue to work with the group on its goals, reformulate the goals, or even sometimes to withdraw from the process.

Rothman (1979) described a particular model of community practice as the social action approach and noted that it was more widely used by practitioners in the past than at the time of writing. However, in some respects the social action model is currently assuming renewed popularity. Increasingly, recent professional literature reports that this type of model is being used by practitioners with task groups (Home, 1991; Mondros & Berman-Rossi, 1991; Mullender & Ward, 1991; Sachs, 1991).

The social action model assumes that disadvantaged and oppressed populations need to be organized to pressure power holders to redistribute goods and wealth in a more equitable manner. In these situations the practitioner works with and educates the oppressed to empower them to negotiate, advocate, and demand in order to bring about the needed changes. Changes that are expected to affect the members directly may also bring about needed changes for others in similar circumstances. An example of this type of social interaction is described by Sachs (1991) for work with homeless people. A small group of homeless persons were empowered to develop a shelter for themselves and for others who needed this resource.

CONCLUSION

In this chapter, the large issue of the relationship between task and emotion in groups was considered, both in regard to types of groups and in relation to interaction within groups. Of seven types of task groups subsequently discussed (including committees, which were discussed as ubiquitous, even prototypical task groups), two—teams and administrative groups—bear special relationship to this issue. Although teams were noted for their emphasis on social-emotional or maintenance aspects as well as their task orientation, administrative groups were featured for their importance in the functioning and survival of most social agencies.

We noted two other types of task groups, focus groups and social action groups, that currently receive special attention from many practitioners. Focus groups, which have received renewed consideration lately, were discussed as important task groups linking research and practice. Social action groups were also considered important for their resurgent use among task groups and for their potential to help members as well as those in the members' social environment.

Delegate councils were emphasized for their contribution to the democratic aspects of task groups. Both social action groups and delegate councils consider and reflect significant involvement with the social environment of participants. Treatment conferences were considered in regard to their contribution to improve functioning of clients. It was noted that contemporary versions often incorporate members of the client's social environment as well.

Although more work is needed in order to truly understand these differing types of task groups and their manner of functioning, this chapter has shown the limits of current thinking about categorizing task groups (see Toseland & Rivas, 1994), has noted their limits and exceptions, and to some extent has expanded the framework as well. Some understanding of who, how, and why members come together will help to further clarify conceptualizations about the large variety of task groups. Indeed, the next chapter is focused on what actions are needed in order to plan, compose, and recruit for a task group.

Part II

THE PROFESSIONAL PRACTITIONER'S ROLE IN TASK GROUPS

Chapter 3

PLANNING, COMPOSING, AND RECRUITING A TASK GROUP

The purpose of this chapter is to consider how to plan, compose, and recruit members of task groups. However, let us begin by considering whether an individual or a task group is most appropriate or effective in resolving a problem or producing a product. (See Chapter 7 for a discussion of the effectiveness of group problem solving.) Although many studies have been conducted to resolve this issue, the evidence about the effectiveness of one system over the other is still mixed. In reviewing the research, however, Hare (1976) wrote, "When pairs or larger groups are compared in the solution of the same types of problems, the groups are generally found to be more efficient than individuals" (p. 318). Hare's conclusion is supported by many other studies, including one by Rotter and Portugal (1969).

The greater effectiveness of groups versus individuals is contingent on the nature of the task. For complex tasks, groups tend to be superior to individuals because groups allow for the division of labor (Lorge, 1955). If the task does not require a division of labor and in situations in which problem solution is either correct or incorrect, pairs tend to arrive at more correct answers than do individuals, although groups take longer to solve problems (Barton, 1926; Klugman, 1944). Another consideration is whether the problem solver is average or superior. Hare (1976) pointed out that "although the group is usually better than the average individual, it is seldom better than the best individual" (p. 319).

Other factors also help determine whether the judgment of the individual or the group is superior in decision making. Because the members of a group must deliberate with each other, time is an important factor to take into account. In this regard, group decision making is more costly than individual problem solving. Also, with task groups, a larger number of resources and opinions and a greater amount of knowledge can be taken into account. However, group norms and pressures sometimes prevent the members from expressing their opinions, and the individual's information processing may be inhibited by socioemotional dynamics that occur in the group. (See Chapter 8 for further consideration of decisions and decision making.)

Task groups may have an advantage over the individual because of the fact that people are more willing to accept, support, and implement a decision that is made by a group rather than an individual. "If the solution is going to affect the group and implies change in procedures, the engagement of those who will be affected by the solution may ensure greater acceptance if the members determine the solution" (Hartford, 1972, p. 53). In addition, translation of the problem and of the means of reaching an outcome is not as necessary when a group has been involved.

PLANNING THE TASK GROUP

Once it has been determined that a task group will be useful, planning is essential to its success. Careful attention should be paid to the first set of factors for consideration: the purposes, goals, and expected products and outcomes of the group that will result from the interaction of group members. As these factors are clearly and specifically identified, further planning for the group can be accomplished.

Purposes, Goals, and Expected Products and Outcomes

The practitioner's clear thinking and understanding concerning the expected purpose, product, and outcomes expected are essential to the planning process. If the purpose of the group is to plan and organize a communitywide fund-raising drive for the children's wing of the community hospital, the membership for this planning committee will probably be rather small and carefully selected. The following persons may be especially desirable as members: (a) a physician working closely with the children in the hospital; (b) a person who has contacts with newspaper, radio, and television personnel; (c) a well-liked and influential member of the community; (d) a person with knowledge and experience in planning community events; (e) a person with good mediation skills; (f) someone with fund-raising skills; and (g) others with special skills, knowledge, and influence of use in accomplishing the task. Because specific member characteristics are desirable, recruitment requires direct individual contact with selected potential members.

In the above example, the purposes, products, and outcomes clearly affect who is selected for membership on the committee, how the members are selected and recruited, and the size of the group. Other factors that may be determined by these beginning decisions are the expected duration of the group, the agency sponsorship, the meeting place, the type of interaction expected among members, and the way the group is organized, including whether the chairperson is an agency staff person, a group member appointed by an agency staff person, or a person to be elected by the group.

In contrast to the situation described above, if the goal is to develop community awareness and beginning problem solving, factors such as membership, recruitment, agency affiliation, group size, and meeting place will differ greatly. A person living in a community may determine that the children in that area require a variety of services. The expected outcomes are community awareness of this as a problem and some beginning plans for resolving this problem. Membership will be the basis of the interest and motivation of those living in the community and of their willingness to attend the sessions. Recruitment could probably be accomplished by placing signs in neighborhood windows of businesses and homes and in public places. The signs might say "Save Our Children!" and include a time, date, and place for a meeting. It is important that the meeting place be large, physically available, and acceptable to those expected to attend.

Other factors that warrant careful thinking through and planning are the social context, structure, size, and duration of the group; the timing and frequency of meetings; physical environment; group composition; and recruitment methods.

Social Context

The social context of the task group includes its agency or community affiliation. In many instances, the social context is predetermined by the fact that an executive or another person in the social agency makes the decision to appoint a committee, thereby automatically using that setting as the context for the group. The task group thus becomes intrinsically linked to the functioning of the agency, resulting in pressures to conform to the agency's policies and procedures. (See Chapter 6 for more discussion of social pressures in task groups.)

Often, however, choices exist about the affiliation of a task group, which is an important consideration because group goals are frequently influenced by their surrounding culture. "The pervasive values and norms of the society, the community or the institutional context within which the group is established will frequently condition the group goals and objectives" (Hartford, 1972, p. 152). Task groups accrue benefits by affiliating themselves with organizations whose missions are congruent with their own. Often, agency resources are made available to the task group, including the services of a relatively high-status staff member. The task group assesses the social agency or organization, which also has a purpose for sanctioning the task group. To facilitate this process, it is often appropriate to write a proposal regarding the task group to be presented to the agency administrators. In planning for the group, the worker considers the fit between the sponsoring body (agency, organization, or community) and the proposed group.

Structure

Some elements of group structure must be decided on before major planning can be accomplished. An initial decision is whether an organizer (staff or community person) is going to do the basic planning regarding group organization or whether the planning will be conducted later by the members. In either case, certain decisions are essential. After having reviewed the purpose of the group, the size, and other elements of the composing process, an initial decision is made regarding structure and organization that will be the most conducive to producing the desired outcomes.

Two basic types of task group structures, informal and formal, exist. The informal group, in which there are no officially designated roles, is a fairly unusual way to structure task groups. In appointing a committee, usually the chairperson is named, even when the other members of the group are not named. When the committee members are not specifically named, the task of member selection is usually expected to be accomplished by the chairperson. This type of organization would probably typify an ad hoc committee, which is short term and very specific in purpose.

In a neighborhood or community-change task group, several persons with similar concerns usually come together to begin work on a problem area. Initially, no one may be designated as the chairperson or leader; as the group meets for the purpose of organization, the leadership role emerges from the interaction among the members.

As the task group develops to a more formalized type of organization with leadership elected by the members, several factors affect the members' movement toward more formal role designations and more organization. These changes occur as needs of members are identified and as the members understand that organization facilitates goal achievement. Other factors that affect goal structure are the size of the group and physical environment.

In the task group there is a great variation in the amount of formal structure that may be determined even before the group meets for the first time. "In highly formalized groups there may be detailed written statements concerning the structure. The bylaws of an organization may specify all the positions within it together with the duties of each as well as the types of relationships expected among them" (Cartwright & Zander, 1960, p. 645). This type of organization gives order and direction to the life of the group. Evidence of this type of formal structure is usually very visible because it is often recorded on the group's organizational chart.

Even in this very formal group structure, an informal structure will emerge from the members' interactions over time. Such informal structure can be an obstruction to the accomplishment of the group purpose, or it can be helpful in moving the group more successfully in the designated direction.

Size

The size of the task group is another factor that is determined in the planning process. A useful guideline is: "The group should be small enough to allow it to accomplish its purpose, and yet large enough to permit members to have a satisfying experience" (Toseland & Rivas, 1984, p. 126). The optimal size depends on the purpose of the group and the attributes of the members.

As task groups increase in size, some characteristics are taken into consideration. For instance, as size increases, members tend to establish formal rules and regulations, and the group becomes more like a formal organization than a small group (Shepherd, 1964). An increase in size leads to a decrease in cohesion, a requirement for the division of labor, and the formation of subgroups (Thomas & Fink, 1963).

An increase in size brings certain advantages to the task group. A larger group provides a broader range of abilities, knowledge, and skills, as well as a greater number of "hands" to accomplish the task. One might also expect better problem-solving effectiveness in a larger group, which tends to have a greater variety of resources available for problem solving than a smaller one. Such resources include a greater number of items of information that can be absorbed and recalled, more judgments available to correct errors of information and inference, more ideas for problem solution, a greater range of values and technical skills, and more power to implement the decisions.

Changes in the size of the task group are often related to changes in the satisfaction of the members. As the number of potential relationships increases rapidly, there is greater emotional demand on the members and a necessity for greater coordination of the many factors in the group that affect the members. There is a demand for each individual to respond to more member, dyadic, and triadic relationships. Slater (1955) noted that "in large groups physical freedom is restricted while psychological freedom is increased. The member has less time to talk, more points of view to integrate and adapt to, and a more elaborate structure into which to fit" (p. 138). In reviewing the literature in this area, Golembiewski (1962) postulated that if the size of the group is increased, the most active participants become more active, whereas the least active participants become less active and may even become silent. Zimet and Schneider (1969) found that in most groups a few members do most of the talking. There were more reports of feelings of threat or inhibition of impulse as the size of the group increased. Shaw (1976) noted that some interpersonal needs might be better met in larger groups. For most people, one of the advantages of larger groups is that they provide more opportunities for meeting interesting, attractive people and for rewarding interaction to occur. For the shy person, large groups provide more anonymity.

Some researchers have attempted to identify an optimum size for the task group. Brilhart (1974) suggested that the most common size for a committee was five, seven, or nine members. Hare (1952) found that five was an optimum size for member satisfaction. Zastrow (1985) indicated that perhaps because of the formation of subgroups, groups with an even number of members have more disagreements and conflicts than do odd number groups. A useful principle is "the least group size," which states that the proper size of the group is the "smallest group in which it is possible to have represented at a functional level all of the social and achievement skills required for the particular activity" (Thelen, 1954, pp. 187-188).

Duration of the Group

Can the task be accomplished in a relatively brief period of time, or will this be a group that will continue indefinitely? The response to this question indicates that duration is another important consideration in planning for a task group. Indeed, it often is a crucial factor in a potential member's determination about participating in a group. "If one has questions about joining a group, serving on a committee, associating or working with people who are not necessarily to his liking, such an assignment may be palatable to the person if he knows that he can escape in a short time, because of the short duration of the group" (Hartford, 1972, p. 183).

Merton (1957) stated that the self-selection of members, the quality and quantity of involvement, the structure, and other properties of the task group are affected by whether the group is short or long term. In the short-term group, members' perceptions that the group is separate from their real lives affect the group process. Trust, experimentation, responding to the novelty of the group, and productiveness are likely to be characteristics of time-limited, temporary groups. Members of short-term groups usually take more risks and endure more discomforts than members of long-term groups. In contrast, members who participate in long-term task groups are inclined and encouraged to invest themselves in group membership in major ways (Ephross & Vassil, 1987).

Timing and Frequency of Group Meetings

Timing is another important consideration in planning a task group. Obviously the time set for the sessions is an important factor for members in terms of their attendance. Potential members may have broad constraints on their ability to participate. Populations of persons who are desirable as members should be identified and the meeting time matched as closely as possible to their availability. For example, to reach a group of young mothers who were staying at home and caring for their young children, we might schedule the group session at 10:00 a.m. and provide child care for the children during this time. Sometimes, as member recruitment begins or even after the group begins, the time may be reconsidered and changed as needed. If we were primarily interested in reaching persons who were employed, we probably would schedule the group in the evening. Other important considerations may be the timing of other committees and service clubs and special community events that have already been scheduled.

Frequency of the meetings varies greatly among task groups. Usually, small groups and subcommittees of large social agencies are very flexible in terms of frequency of meetings. When there is a demand for intensity in work, the task group is likely to meet often. As the demand is met and the pressure subsides, the group may go back to its previous regular schedule.

In contrast, many formal long-term groups meet regularly at a set time on a predetermined schedule.

Location and Physical Environment

Another factor for consideration in planning a task group is the place and physical environment of the task group. Although many task group organizers perceive this as a relatively unimportant issue, several studies indicate that this is an exceedingly important area for careful planning (Mehrabian & Diamond, 1971; Minz, 1956). "Groups are embedded in a complex environmental setting that exerts a strong influence in almost every aspect of group process" (Shaw, 1976, p. 113). The structural elements of space are seen by Hartford (1972) as affecting size, composition, location, and physical arrangement, which in turn affect member interactions. The location of the task group is important in that the group must be in a position to make a difference. For instance, a task group that is attempting to influence a particular political leader certainly should be within the leader's political jurisdiction.

Ecological space is very important to task group members. Leaders need to consider how far potential members will travel to participate in task groups. How will concerns about safety in the neighborhood after dark affect attendance at meetings? Will some people refuse to attend because of the perceived bureaucratic nature of the agency where the task group is to meet? Are there negative factors within the building that affect the desire or ability to participate, such as the requirement to walk a long distance, ride an elevator, or walk up many flights of stairs?

Meeting in the same place over a period of time usually contributes to the creation of cohesion in the task group. "A constant location reinforces the consciousness of group" (Hartford, 1972, p. 173). Although task groups tend to be relatively focused on the task, many members develop a sense of home at such meetings. People who spend long periods of time in the same environment get used to certain smells, noises, location of facilities, and chair arrangements, resulting in what Sommer (1969) called "institutional sanctity" (p. 34).

COMPOSING THE TASK GROUP

In order to plan the composition of a task group, one must utilize the factors that are necessary to accomplish a specific purpose, including group cohesion, member motivation, knowledge and skills of members, ability to represent a population of interest, and sphere of influence. The individuals who make up a task group are a powerful determinant of the group's behavior and process. Organizing a group requires a determination of the most advantageous balance in factors to produce the most effective answers or solution, the best product, or the most favorable outcome. The specific group qualities and characteristics that are most conducive to producing the most desirable outcomes must be determined.

Group Attractiveness

A very basic characteristic is group attractiveness, which emphasizes the importance of cohesion even in the beginning of the task group. Literature on short-term groups suggests that attraction to the group is related to the content of the session rather than to the other members, resulting from their interacting together (Alissi & Casper, 1985). The purpose of the task group and the broad goals should be made explicit from the very beginning, so that potential members will be clear about the purpose and tasks to be accomplished. Concomitantly, leaders are aware that a change in focus may occur as the group comes together and the members modify some of their thinking and planning.

Leaders are concerned about the attractiveness of the group at its beginning and want the task group to retain the elements of cohesion for as long as it takes to accomplish its tasks. Therefore, some thinking and planning is to be done about the long-term consequences for the task group with a particular combination of members. This type of attraction to the group, or cohesion, is "the resultant of all the forces acting on members to remain in the group" (Festinger, Schachter, & Back, 1950, p. 274).

Many studies have found that there is a positive relationship between attraction to the task group and high productivity (Goodacre, 1951; Hemphill & Sechrest, 1952; Roby, 1952; Shaw & Shaw, 1962; Speroff & Kerr, 1952; Strupp & Hausman, 1953; Van Zelst, 1952a). In general, highly cohesive task groups communicate with each other more, are positively oriented, and work harder to achieve the group goals than less cohesive groups (Shaw, 1976).

Member satisfaction is very important to the success of task groups. Studies have indicated that group cohesion is positively related to member satisfaction (Exline, 1959; Gross, 1956; Marquis, Guetzkow, & Heyns, 1951; Van Zelst, 1952b). As a result of cohesion, members have been found to be more energetic, less likely to be absent, and happier when the group succeeds. Although it is evident from the studies cited previously that group cohesion is important in establishing successful working task groups, relatively little research is available about specific predictable factors that produce those results.

Member Characteristics

Member characteristics affect task group interaction and influence outcomes. Although findings regarding member characteristics are often mixed, it is important that the practitioner attempt to use knowledge in this area of practice as much as possible. Task groups should be homogeneous to ensure stability and heterogeneous to produce vitality.

A research consensus exists about the desirability of a range of personality variables of the task group members. Studies indicate that groups that are heterogeneous in regard to personality profiles of the members are more effective than groups in which members have a more homogeneous profile.

Two types of member characteristics, gender and ethnic identity, have recently been studied to attempt to better understand their effects on task group functioning (Davis, 1986; Reed & Garvin, 1983). Even when the specific member factors have been carefully balanced, the leader is still unable to do much more than speculate about the task group members' ability to function together and about their level of cohesiveness. Shaw (1976) used the term *assembly effect* to refer to "variations in group behaviors that are a consequence of the particular combination of persons in the group, apart from the effects produced by the specific characteristics of group members" (p. 195).

Leaders can plan ways to bolster cohesion and to make and keep group participation attractive. Throughout the life of the group, content and success in accomplishing tasks provide the broadest and most important elements for attraction.

Motivation

Another factor important to the accomplishment of group tasks is motivation, which "may be viewed as a force that impels the individual towards, or repels him from, conditions, events, objects, or people" (Patton & Giffin, 1973, p. 12). As a force, motivation is experienced in diverse ways, as an attraction to the purpose and tasks and later as a member of that body.

Individuals who are motivated primarily by social needs desire friendships, acceptance, attention, and belonging. Related themes are intimacy and distance, personal attractiveness and popularity, and norms and standards of social and sexual behavior. These factors in a task group would attract members who have these desires.

Those persons who tend to be motivated by competence regularly consider achievement, productivity, understanding, and creativity. They would be attracted to task groups that allow or encourage this type of participation. Typical themes related to competence motivation include conflicts over facts, opinions, plans, and theories.

Knowledge and Skill

Another important factor in composing a task group is the knowledge and skill of the potential members. In order to act as a resource for the group, members must possess facts and information and have access to obtaining knowledge. Members of a task group should "possess all the information necessary to the performance of their task plus the ability to interpret and use it" (Scheidel & Crowell, 1979, p. 122).

An additional area of skill that is invaluable to the task group is the potential member's ability to interact with others within the group process. Leaders assess whether members are able to assume roles that are beneficial to the group in resolving conflicts.

In task groups whose purpose is social action, it is especially important that the members "be able to function well enough as individuals and collectively to constitute a group that provides a unified force for action" (Hartford, 1972, p. 54). A split in opinions of members about action to be taken can produce a decision that carries minimal commitment from the members. The majority of the members may have voted for the decision but only by a slight margin of one or two votes. Because social action groups usually intend to bring about some change in a system outside the group, this lack of real commitment is going to weaken any driving force for change. In the instance of the community that was attempting to serve the children residing there, the group agreed that indeed there was a problem but expressed opposing views of how the problem could be resolved, thereby weakening the force required to bring about change. The members may have voted by a simple majority to act on a plan. The opposition by the rest of the task group may create a conflict that consumes the energy of the members to act on the decision.

Other group processes are important in social change groups and are taken into account in composing such a group. Because of the resistance that is often a reaction to change, the group must be sufficiently synthesized to support its members. "The group must provide rewards for members from within the group if their proposed change means deviance from the wider social system and the possibilities of negative social sanctions in the wider society or external system" (Hartford, 1972, p. 54). This point is illustrated in an agency that developed a committee to rid the neighborhood of drug dealers. One member lived in that community and knew that most others living there hated the police more than the dealers. The solution decided on in the task group, regardless of community opinion, was to have police institute foot patrols. When returning to the neighborhood, the member might be harassed by friends and neighbors about this decision. In order for that member to remain in that group despite the attitude of the community, he or she must receive personally important rewards from the other committee members in the form of special support, thanks from the other members, increased status within the group, or other indirect ways.

In some situations, the task group members' knowledge and skills are combined with the acceptance of members by the population of interest. A task group member may be perceived by that population as a leader in that community or among those persons or at least as having knowledge and shared experiences with that group of the population, thus providing a link with a specific segment of people. For example, a woman's health clinic might realize that unmarried women were not making use of the services. The clinic could include an unmarried adult woman on a planning group in order to make connections with the population that was not being adequately served.

Often task groups require members who, in addition to providing feedback from a specific population that they wish to serve, also communicate in ways that influence that population. In counseling adolescent boys and girls about AIDS, administrative committee members who have lines of communication to that population can influence their behavior and help them realize how they can benefit from such services.

Although planning and composing a task group are not yet thoroughly scientific, the findings of many studies influence the decisions and behaviors of leaders in forming task groups. After the planning has been carefully done and the areas of composition have been thoughtfully determined, the next step is the recruitment of the group members.

RECRUITING THE TASK GROUP MEMBERS

Recruitment involves securing the services of individuals. Motivation may be the most important characteristic of members. Useful in accomplishing a task is a group of individuals who wish to accomplish what this group intends to do. For example, some neighborhood residents decided that they must do something to rid their area of drug dealers. Once it had been determined that motivation was a primary desired characteristic for the task group members, the residents used a recruitment method of posting signs around the neighborhood publicizing the organization of this group so that those persons motivated to participate would join.

Obviously, when it is determined that motivation is the most important member characteristic, other characteristics usually considered in the formation of a task group are very limited. Indeed, in this example, about the only other member distinctiveness that can be expected with this method of recruitment is that the individuals are expected to come from the same geographic area and, therefore, possibly of the same ethnic or racial background. If this form of recruitment is used, some factors related to composition are predictable, although others are not.

The only way the important member characteristics can be initially controlled is by purposeful recruitment. Furthermore, the decisions made in the thinking-through process are connected with the methods of recruitment for members. The way in which such decisions influence recruitment is illustrated in the following examples. A small agency located in a very large building with other social service organizations was assigned three parking spaces for staff member use. Those employees not assigned one of the spaces had to park a block away from the building. The agency staff consisted of an executive director, seven social workers, two nurses, and four secretaries. Initially, all of the staff wanted the luxury of such easy parking. Certainly the executive director could make these assignments, but would all of the cogent facts be taken into account and would the decisions be acceptable to the staff? The director decided to appoint a committee to undertake this task. The fact that the decisions were made by a number of people would help the others abide by the decisions reached.

In order to make this decision even more acceptable, it was important to have the different professional units represented on the committee. This requirement is based on the fact that the work demands might differ for the various units. For example, the nurses and secretaries generally remained in the building all day, although each of the social workers brought clients to the building at least three times a day. The executive director was also aware of the fact that both males and females were employed in each of the professional units. As a result of this analysis of the situation, the director appointed a committee made up of representatives of each of the professional units, attempting to apportion the number of representatives as equitably as possible. She was also aware of the skills of the members in functioning cooperatively in a task group. In this instance, recruitment or securing services involved only the person responsible for naming the persons to participate.

In another example, it was determined that although Native Americans were living in a community with a medical clinic, they were underutilizing the services. The clinic administrator asked the social services practitioner to develop a committee to turn this situation around. It was important to be clear about the purpose of the group. The desired outcome was the use of the clinic services by the Native Americans. Because the practitioner did not know why they were not coming for services, it was first very important to understand the possible reasons for the lack of service utilization. As a result, members of the Native American group who could represent the culture and views of the people and also influence the thinking of their peers were recruited. Representation from doctors was also important in order to help the physicians understand these potential clients and for the Native Americans to make direct connections with the persons who would be giving services. Other important members to be represented were well-known, well-regarded, and influential members of the majority culture so that the participation of the Native Americans in the clinic would be seen as desirable by the majority users.

After the practitioner has determined the many important and necessary decisions regarding the group, such as size, place of meeting, and the specific membership desired (with a few notions of alternative members), the actual recruitment begins. In such a situation it may be very important to think about the individuals to make the direct approach to the desired members. There may be an administrative board whose members already have some acquaintance with the potential members. These persons would probably be the most influential individuals to approach the potential new members. If this structure does not exist then the practitioner may use his or her contacts in the community to begin to make connections with the potential committee members. It is generally agreed that personal contact rather than contact by phone is likely to be more successful in recruiting new members.

During contacts with potential members, two areas are most important for the recruiter's attention. One is the broad area of assessment, focused on the potential of this individual to become a valuable, cooperative, functioning member of a task group with a given purpose and composed of other specific individuals. The other major area of concern is the strength of motivation for the individual to participate in this group. To recruit effectively, the practitioner should make use of knowledge concerning the source of motivation and attempt to strengthen that force sufficiently for the individual to accept membership in the group.

CONCLUSION

To maximize the success of a task group, it is important that the practitioner use all the knowledge available in guiding the process of group development. The success of a task group is based initially on the planning, composition, and appropriate recruitment of the members who will participate. Factors to be considered in planning include social context; group structure; group size; duration of the group; timing and frequency of group meetings; and location and physical environment of meetings. Planning for group composition involves a consideration of group attractiveness and of individual characteristics, including their motivation, knowledge, and skills. Motivation of potential members is also an important consideration for recruitment of group members. This chapter has focused on task groups in general. The next chapter highlights a particular type of task group that is an important part of contemporary social services: the team.

Chapter 4

THE PROFESSIONAL'S ROLE ON THE SOCIAL SERVICE TEAM

The objective of the present chapter is to consider the nature, purposes, and functions of social service teams as specialized task groups with their own small group processes and development. Teams are organized task groups (Toseland & Rivas, 1984) composed of persons from differing professions or of differing specialists from the same profession who work together using structured activities, processes, and procedures. Teams are defined as organizational work groups or administrative groups consisting of staff members who are devoted to task accomplishment within an organization, whose work is generally sanctioned by a sponsoring agency (Fiorelli, 1988). Social service teams are devoted to accomplishing social service tasks (Compton & Galaway, 1984). In addition to focusing on their tasks, successful teams attend to their process (Haines & McKeachie, 1982). Moreover, the work of teams is intended to benefit clients (Brown, 1991) and to have broader benefits for the clients' family members, team members and leaders, the social service organization, and the wider society.

Teams are prevalent in social service organizations. The goals and objectives of teams, which are related to the mission of the social agency, are determined by the team members (Henry, 1992). Furthermore, teams are subject to accountability demands and standards of effective performance that tend to be measured objectively and operationally as outcomes (Fandt, Cady, & Sparks, 1993).

PURPOSES AND FUNCTIONS OF TEAMS

Underlying team functioning is an egalitarian philosophy that implies that the contributions of all team members are based on professional authority and are valuable (Heap, 1977). In some social agencies supervision is carried out with an egalitarian, collegial, and leaderless team approach (Shulman, 1982). However, on many teams there are tensions that reflect the contrast between an egalitarian philosophy and the realities of differential status and power accorded to professions and among team members (Hall, 1986). For example, during a team meeting a member of a relatively low-status profession verbalized the expectation that his contribution was meaningful; other members reacted with bemusement, surprise, and impatience. Afterward, the member was told by another member that it was naive to believe that all were equal on this particular team. Furthermore, members of mental health teams tend to disagree about whether team members should be equal in power (Toseland, Palmer-Ganeles, & Chapman, 1986).

The key functions of teams are decision making and problem solving. (See Chapter 7 for more about problem solving and Chapter 8 for more about decision making.) Indeed, many teams are designed to make decisions and deliver social services. Teams are trusted to make significant decisions that are central to the purpose of the organization and that supersede and thereby carry more weight than the decisions that any one professional (with the exception of an executive) within one organization is usually required to make. Well-functioning social service teams often produce higher quality decisions than an individual; however, under some circumstances, such as that of groupthink in which social pressures interfere with rational processes, this does not occur. (See Chapter 6 for further discussion of this problem.) For most teams, decision making about both internal matters, such as improving team functioning, and external matters, namely, those outside of the purview of the team itself, is a common activity (Henry, 1992).

TEAMS AND ORGANIZATIONS

Team Formation and Organizational Roles

Teams are often created to meet the needs of clients in an accountable manner. Indeed, discussions are used as a means of getting input from clients (Compton & Galaway, 1984). An evaluation of the team's effectiveness in fulfilling its functions reveals the necessity of its continuation.

The roles of the team member vary according to his or her role in the organization and the characteristics of the team's organizational environment. In organizations in which a particular social service profession predominates, the role of the member of that profession is likely to be more influential than in host agencies, in which the member of that profession has less influence. For example, the social worker is likely to have more influence on a child welfare team than on a hospital team.

Members of teams have role assignments (Shaver & Buhrmester, 1984), and social-emotional and task roles are usually differentiated within teams (Henry, 1992). For effective team functioning members must be flexible and be willing and able to engage in role negotiation (Compton & Galaway, 1984). For example, the leader of a public welfare social services team was absent on the day of a crucial team meeting. Another member of the team, who ordinarily did not function in an active leadership role and who was not particularly vocal during meetings, rounded up the team members and informally functioned as team leader with the tacit and somewhat surprised compliance of the other members.

The formal and informal positions and power of the team members are often directly related to their positions and power within the organization. However, in some situations, team members with little formal power may have a great deal of informal power stemming from years of experience. For instance, on a social service delivery team, two members of a profession with relatively little occupational prestige nevertheless commanded a great deal of attention and respect because of their thorough knowledge of the child care institution and its history and their effectiveness in accomplishing tasks. Relationships with more powerful persons in or out of the team are significant also. For instance, one team member was able to maintain significant power on the team because of the member's close relationships with powerful sponsors of the social service organization.

Titles bear some relationship to the status and prestige of team members and therefore bear some emotional and tangible significance for them, too. However, on some teams members may have titles that convey an impression of great responsibility yet are largely ceremonial.

Professionals and Agencies

Team functioning is influenced by professional and agency cultures (Compton & Galaway, 1984). Professional and agency cultures that are consonant with working collaboratively with other professions are likely to support teamwork, whereas cultures that emphasize autonomy and competitive relationships are likely to interfere with harmonious team functioning. Interdisciplinary professional training, which forms a basis for interprofessional culture, tends to promote teamwork if the contributions of other professions are valued (Courtnage & Smith-Davis, 1987; Payne, 1982).

The attitudes and beliefs of professionals influence the organizational process of teams as well as the effectiveness of their functioning within and among agencies. When trust and respect exist among professionals and among agencies, an important step is taken toward the development of effective teamwork (Compton & Galaway, 1984). If such vital human commodities are lacking, the team becomes an exercise in autocracy in which a single person exercises dictatorial control, thereby making it unnecessary for the other team members to contribute to making a decision rather than merely implementing it. In such situations, members should use the power of the group to make it a more effectively functioning team. For instance, in one outpatient mental health setting, team deliberations were directed by a medical staff member who made significant contributions. However, the staff member alienated the other members by disparaging their contributions and refusing to consider their suggestions. The result was that virtually all team members, although continuing to attend meetings, became silent. Eventually, the members began talking informally between meetings about the team process and decided to support one another and to pay less attention to the suggestions of the medical staff member.

Fields of Practice

Teams are useful in practice, policy, and research (Toseland & Rivas, 1984). The particular field of practice is essential in determining the team dynamics, structure, and composition and the role of the team member. Some fields of practice that utilize social service teams include health, mental health, education, public welfare, family counseling, rehabilitation, and social planning (Ducanis & Golin, 1979; Heap, 1977). For example, in mental health teams the role of the social worker includes being knowledgeable about the social context of clients' lives, their family and community relationships, and available material resources and social services.

The field of practice of the team influences the relationships among the professionals who compose the team. In mental health treatment teams, psychiatrists often seek to enlist the collaboration of social workers and other professionals prior to inaugurating psychopharmacological interventions

Table 4.1

Typology of Social Service Teams

	Organization	
Discipline	Intraorganizational	Interorganizational
Unidisciplinary	a	b
Multidisciplinary	c	d

(Waldinger, 1990). Child protection teams often seek out medical consultants to help them interpret medical information, review medical records, and conduct physical examinations (Gray & Fryer, 1991).

Types of Teams

The role of the professional on the team varies as a function of the type of team. Teams may be conceptualized on two dimensions, organization and discipline, each of which contains two categories, between and within, as follows. Teams are either intraorganizational or interorganizational and unidisciplinary or multidisciplinary, as shown in Table 4.1.

The four resulting cells of the conceptualization are as follows: The intraorganizational-unidisciplinary category *a* is the simplest type. An example is a team composed entirely of social workers within one public welfare agency.

The next two categories of team types are intermediate in complexity. An example of the interorganizational-unidisciplinary category *b* is a team composed entirely of social workers from different agencies who meet to work on issues of child sexual abuse. An example of the intraorganizational-multidisciplinary category *c* is a team composed of allied health professionals in a hospital.

The interorganizational-multidisciplinary category *d* is the most complex type of team. An example is a team composed of representatives of a range of helping professions from a variety of community agencies who coordinate their efforts to combat juvenile delinquency.

Interdisciplinary and Multidisciplinary Teams

Collaboration between members of different professions entails understanding the socialization of other professions, including their priorities, values, and treatment models (Abramson, 1993). Variation exists between and even within the helping professions in regard to their use of the medical model as compared with holistic and ecological models (Kay, Moffatt, MacTavish, & Lau, 1990).

Interdisciplinary teams are composed of professionals such as social workers, psychologists, teachers, guidance and educational counselors, marital and family counselors, substance abuse counselors, nurses, physical and occupational therapists, psychiatrists and other medical professionals, attorneys, and paraprofessionals (Toseland & Rivas, 1984). Of course, any given team will consist of a sample of professionals rather than the entire range. The actual composition of the interdisciplinary team is dependent on the purpose of the team, the agencies represented, the availability of personnel, political considerations, and the size of the team. Each profession, of course, has its area of expertise. For example, on infertility treatment teams the social worker's role is that of counselor and educator (Greenfeld, Diamond, Breslin, & DeCherney, 1986). The team member's profession and area of expertise are likely to have specific beneficial consequences for the team. For instance, early childhood intervention teams that have social workers as regular team members tend to have higher levels of parental involvement than other teams (Nash, Rounds, & Bowen, 1992).

In contrast to multidisciplinary teamwork, interdisciplinary teamwork is characterized by shared purpose, creative problem solving, and synergy in which combined activities result in a product that is greater than the individual components (Fiorelli, 1988). Interdisciplinary teamwork includes multidisciplinary composition and participation yet transcends it through the sharing of information in a collaborative manner, coordination of activities, and input by group members into the decision-making and goal-setting processes. In practice, many teams that are labeled interdisciplinary function in a multidisciplinary manner (Bennett, 1982). In multidisciplinary teams, areas of expertise and intervention that are separate and those that are overlapping should be defined so that the role of each team member is clear. For instance, on a mental health team functioning in outpatient and consultation settings, the role of the social worker is that of expert in family assessment and treatment, and the role of the clinical nurse specialist is that of supportive therapist and liaison with the nursing staff (Leigh, 1987).

Often members of interdisciplinary teams perceive themselves as primarily representing their own profession (Sands, Stafford, & McClelland, 1990). Indeed, in interdisciplinary teams, the role of the team members includes presenting the viewpoints of their professions on the issue at hand. For example, the social worker on the team is likely to present a generalist perspective, an understanding of the social context, and a concern for issues of social justice, oppression, and discrimination.

Occasionally, because of the field of practice setting and their audience on the team, some team members identify with and profess the values of other professions. For instance, a social worker who was a member of a pupil personnel team tended to present views from an educational and psychological perspective.

Although individual functioning is important, it is the collective functioning of teams that contributes to their effectiveness (Henry, 1992). For instance, by working together, a child sexual abuse team increased its comfort level in reporting suspected cases, became more thorough in coordinating investigation and treatment activities, and improved its ability to educate the general public about the problem of child sexual abuse (Wagner, 1987). In another instance, a child protection team used a team approach to counter the passive, aggressive, hopeless, and challenging resistance to treatment by abusing families (Morrison, 1987). The team conducted assessment sessions of the marital, parent-child, and sibling subsystems and decided on children's return to their families in team conferences.

Numerous obstacles present within the team as well as within its organizational context, including leadership, goals, communications, and intrateam relationships, have the potential to impede the effective functioning of interdisciplinary teams (Chafetz, West, & Ebbs, 1987). For adequate team functioning, institutions and organizations should have a philosophy and reward system that supports interdisciplinary activity, provides a commitment to staffing the team, allocates resources such as physical space, allows the team the power to control its own procedures, and supports the team's domain of authority and expertise, thereby maintaining its decision-making options (Abramson, 1989; Watt, 1985). Leadership should address task issues involving the activities as well as the socioemotional maintenance of the team. Goal setting requires an integrated evaluation of data collected by members, as well as members who are competent and not overwhelmed by stress and burnout.

Relationships within the team can help foster a sense of unity and cohesiveness that will provide team members with the power to function effectively (Garner, 1988). Although the helping professions share a great deal, their fragmentation has led to considerable conflict and rivalry that hamper the efficiency of teamwork (Compton & Galaway, 1984).

An obstacle to effective interdisciplinary teamwork is feeling helpless when confronted with the power and authority of another profession. For example, a psychologist who was a member of an interdisciplinary mental health team was confounded and frustrated by a dominant psychiatrist.

A related obstacle to interdisciplinary teamwork is defining the parameters of one's profession as a domain that should be protected. For example, a marital and family counselor on a treatment team was perturbed when a licensed professional counselor was asked to join in order to help with substance abuse issues. One does not expect members of the helping professions to abandon concerns about turf. However, a greater willingness to be less defensive within the team itself is likely to improve the functioning of the team.

TEAM FUNCTIONING AND SMALL GROUP PROCESSES

Leadership

Teams consist of leaders, who are responsible for overall team functioning (Toseland & Rivas, 1984), and members, who are responsible for participating on the team. On some teams the leader is designated, assigned, or appointed by the agency sponsoring the team (Henry, 1992). Other teams, including many that are involved in carrying out their own team building, have a leader who is drawn from within the team and is elected by the members. Some teams operate without a formally designated leader and use a rotating peer leadership system.

The functions of the team leader include conducting meetings, motivating members, and coordinating the efforts and activities of individual members (Toseland & Rivas, 1984). The leader's functions also include being accountable to the sponsoring agency for the team activities. The leader expends considerable effort in maintaining the team as a unified group and ensuring that the social-emotional needs of members are fulfilled. Team members assume leadership functions as well.

Team Building

A major function of the team leader is team building, which consists of simultaneously working with the team members and with the group as a whole to develop the members' capacities to work together as a group despite inevitable professional and personal differences (Toseland & Rivas, 1984). In team building a considerable amount of cohesion, consisting of normative structure, group culture, and values is useful for setting and achieving the goals of the team (Henry, 1992). Team building involves the creation of trust, enjoyment, interdependence, mutual respect, and cooperation (Napier & Gershenfeld, 1983). In addition, it involves giving the team permission to examine its own functioning in problem-solving activities. The actual expression of team building activities varies between teams. Team building activities include developing the identity of the team, enhancing pride in the team, developing working relationships and alliances between individual members and subgroups within the team, and fostering positive relationships with the team's external environment.

Membership Composition

Teams are similar to other task groups, including committees, representative councils, boards of directors, and community organization groups, in their formality and their task focus but are different from them in group process, which in turn is influenced by the composition of the group. Teams are composed of staff members, each with his or her own set of knowledge and skills, who are chosen for their varied areas of ability and expertise that they share in a purposeful manner to fulfill differential roles and responsibilities (Compton & Galaway, 1984; Henry, 1992; Toseland & Rivas, 1984). Although team members often have considerable knowledge and positive attitudes, knowledge gaps and ambivalent attitudes and behaviors are also common (Pitts, Jackson, & Wilson, 1990).

Teams tend to focus on the solution of problems through the utilization of the differential capacities of team members (Compton & Galaway, 1984). Indeed, multidisciplinary teams are often formed to deal with difficult problems that are ordinarily within the scope of a primary profession yet have aspects that require the consideration of other professionals. For instance, delays in children's speech and language development are within the purview of the speech therapist; but they also involve such issues as difficulties in the parent-child relationship, the child's emotional development, and the child's learning, which require the specialized knowledge of other disciplines (Cadoret, 1989).

In multidisciplinary teams, the diverse educational and professional backgrounds of the members lead to varied perspectives that consequently are frequently expressed as differing points of view. Although such teams often consist of members who are chosen for having differing professional characteristics that may inherently produce conflict, they have the strengths of combining diverse viewpoints and perspectives for solving difficult problems within and between agencies. However, they are also subject to the limitations and liabilities of the individuals who compose the team.

Teams must be composed of a sufficient number of persons to carry out the work of the team (Henry, 1992). Furthermore, although membership of many teams tends to be fixed and closed for substantial periods of time, most teams inevitably experience change in membership due to staff turnover, attrition, and changes in responsibilities and assignments. On some teams members are not replaceable. However, on other teams, members are replaceable by other members who either fit the particular role, as in job description or professional affiliation, or are seen as being able to provide the expertise required by the team.

Cooperation and Competition

As goal-oriented groups, teams consist of members who, although competing with one another on individual or interdisciplinary bases, strive to cooperate with one another to fulfill the greater purposes of the team because of supraordinate goals. A myth exists that all that is required for effective teamwork is a spirit of cooperation. Although team members are oriented to cooperate in order to improve team performance (Waldinger, 1990), the prevalent problem of competition within teams persists. Team members tend to compete with one another as a result of personal and professional rivalries related to striving for scarce resources, including career advancement, financial reimbursement, power, recognition, status, and prestige. Furthermore, although some agencies promote cooperation among team members, others reward competition, which can intrude on the team process. Some evidence exists that members of Asian, Hispanic, and African American cultures tend to be more cooperative and less competitive than members of Anglo cultures when performing group tasks (Cox, Lobel, & McLeod, 1991). To minimize the deleterious effects of competition within the team, including a loss of efficiency and effectiveness in meeting goals and objectives, cooperation within the team should be encouraged through the inclusion of members from cultures that tend to be cooperative. In health care and perhaps other fields of practice, cooperation can be increased through the use of small teams composed of staff members rather than trainees (Stahelski & Tsukuda, 1990). At times, another useful strategy is to direct inner competition outward to improve the team's performance relative to other teams and groups, although such a strategy must be implemented with care because hazards exist with its use.

Rewards

Effective teams regularly assess the performance of individual members (Haines & McKeachie, 1982) and dispense rewards to promote effective team functioning. Teams in social service organizations are affected by rewards that are related to their performance. The concept and application of rewards are important for understanding and promoting team functioning because rewards are useful in all social agencies and organizations. Research evidence on teams suggests that the effectiveness of reward systems varies according to the degree of specialization of assigned tasks (Fandt et al., 1993).

Teams function under interdependent contractual agreements (Henry, 1992), with interdependence of team members being crucial for effective team functioning (Haines & McKeachie, 1982). Interdependence is inherent in reward structures in that within all three of the following types of reward structures team members are encouraged to work together and help each other complete the task of the team (Fandt et al., 1993). However, for each type of reward structure the basis for providing the reward varies.

An *independent* reward structure is one that provides rewards to individual team members on the basis of their own performance without considering the performance of the other team members. For example, through a performance evaluation each member of a mental health team at a private hospital was rewarded for the care of the client for whom he or she had primary responsibility.

An *interdependent* reward structure is one that provides rewards on the basis of the average score of the team members so that the performance of all members influences the rewards of all. For instance, the members of a group services unit of a family services agency were given the reward of an opportunity to attend a professional conference on the basis of the average of the performance ratings they received from agency supervisors.

A *dependent* reward structure provides rewards on the basis of a product by the entire group. This type does not directly reflect individualized performance per se. For example, a social service team wrote a proposal that was approved, and all members of the team were subsequently rewarded.

Communication

For all teams, sound communication is a vital and necessary aspect of group process (Henry, 1992). Well-functioning teams are ones in which communication is effective. Teams are useful in promoting communication among clients or patients, family members, and health care providers

(Blum & Blum, 1991). Teams tend to improve interagency communication (Selinske, 1981) and are effective means of communicating information about policies, procedures, and interventions (Hamlin, 1991).

Ordinarily, the amount of communication within the team is directly related to the frequency of team meetings. A more frequent meeting schedule with brief intervals between meetings is likely to be related to the occurrence of more communication (Toseland & Rivas, 1984). However, meetings that are scheduled too closely together are likely to become unproductive and conflictual and may result in a reduction in both the quality and amount of communication. Means that are used to promote communication outside of or between meetings, as well as occasionally during meetings, include phone calls, memos, and electronic mail.

Communication adequacy is directly related to the time available to send, receive, and process information. Clarifying differences among the professions in their jargon enhances communication within the team. Encouraging openness helps to overcome status differences among members (Lee, 1980).

In mental health treatment teams, intrateam communication is used to promote an adequate level of client care, enhance client understanding of and compliance with treatment, instill confidence among clients and family members by informing them of efforts by team members to coordinate team efforts on their behalf, and increase implementation of the treatment plan by the team members (Waldinger, 1990). In order to promote such communication, members of mental health treatment teams keep informed about the activities of other clinicians by asking them questions, informing them about their own work with clients, sharing observations with them about clients' responses to particular interventions, consulting with them prior to making changes in clients' treatments and sharing the expectation that they will do the same, and meeting with the treatment team to discuss and remedy any problems in communication (Waldinger, 1990).

DEVELOPMENTAL STAGES OF TEAMS

Teams tend to be involving experiences for members who are required to participate actively in decision-making and problem-solving activities (Shaver & Buhrmester, 1984). Of course, there is some variation between team members in regard to their involvement and participation, with some members, by virtue of their role or for motivational reasons, tending to be more involved than others.

As they develop, teams tend to increase the involvement and participation of their members (Fandt et al., 1993). Also, working relationships tend to develop within the team (Compton & Galaway, 1984). Although teams place little emphasis on psychological intimacy, as members work together they get to know one another better over time and personal closeness and intimacy may develop (Shaver & Buhrmester, 1984).

The development of teams as small groups includes formation, ongoing processes, and ending stages. Member behaviors and roles on the social services team and goal-oriented activities vary according to the stage of development of the team.

Formative Stage

During this preliminary stage the team is planned and begins to take form. Task groups are likely to have input into the development of a new or reformulated team, including addressing the requirement for the team, its objectives and goals, composition, and evaluation. Planning meetings are held and responsibilities are assigned for implementing the team concept and pragmatically arranging and scheduling meetings. During subsequent stages of their development, teams are often involved in planning and sharing activities. Case conferences are useful for purposes of joint planning and joint monitoring (Compton & Galaway, 1984).

Beginning Stage

From an analytical perspective, once the new team is formed with a new membership, the beginning stage occurs in terms of the early interaction of the team and the entry and presence of each team member. However, sometimes one aspect is dynamic and the other static, as in the introduction of one or more new team members to an extant team or the formation of a new team with primarily veteran members who are acquainted with one another and with teamwork. The beginning stage of teamwork is an extended one (Henry, 1992) and consists of two substages, namely, orientation and initial engagement.

Orientation Substage. As part of a larger and broader orientation to working in a social agency (Abramson, 1993), which is often very useful to new employees, persons develop skills in interdisciplinary collaboration and teamwork. The orientation can also be designed for more experienced persons who can benefit from a briefer and more focused orientation that imparts information about the norms of the particular team and inculcates attitudes that will promote teamwork in a particular setting. For new social agency employees, sharing vignettes of collaborative exchanges from process recordings of team meetings and enacting role plays of team process are beneficial methods of furthering their understanding of the importance and means of cooperation on a team. Exchanges that illustrate conflict between team members are also useful when they are placed within a problem-solving context oriented to acquainting new team members with the realities of teamwork.

Initial Engagement Substage. At this point, new team members, as well as team members who have considerable experience with the agency or with teamwork and at most require an abbreviated form of the orientation subphase, enter the initial engagement substage. During the initial engagement substage team members seek to define their position as well as that of others on the team and to gain clarity about the team's purposes and activities. The initial engagement substage is often marked by a period in which members develop working relationships with one another and begin to coalesce as a unit.

Effective leaders motivate the members to join them in promoting the functioning of the team. Knowledge of group dynamics tends to make the beginning stage more manageable for the team leader and members. For instance, a new team leader understood that conflict over positions within and leadership of the group often occurs during the beginning phase and was therefore able to maintain equilibrium when it occurred.

The leader attempts to promote the cohesion of the team and emphasizes its focus on task issues and products. Team-building program media include contract exercises, cohesion exercises, and experiences balancing individual and organizational objectives (Henry, 1992). For example, to build cohesion, the leader of a child protective services team asked each member to think of and share one idea about what they liked about the team.

Middle Stage

The conflicts and issues that emerge during the beginning stage are usually resolved by the middle stage. (However, for a consideration of how conflict among members over power and control that has not been worked out earlier in the group process may interfere with team functioning, see Chapter 6.) For most teams the middle stage is the longest and most productive of the three stages of team functioning. During this stage, which is characterized by work activity, the team is actively involved in address-ing issues, making decisions, and solving problems. In the middle phase the members offer their views, share information, and make assessments as a way of furthering the information-processing, decision-making, and problem-solving functions of the team. Team-sustaining program media include role plays, simulations, trust- and cohesion-building exercises, goal exercises, retreats, marathons, and formalized role-strengthening exercises (Henry, 1992).

Ending Stage

Most teams do not have fixed time limits (Henry, 1992) and may continue with different objectives and changed composition. Because most teams are long-term groups, the ending is usually that of one or a few members leaving the team in a brief and sometimes ritualized ending.

Many organizational work groups, including teams, terminate as an inevitable part of the life cycle of the group, either because of systemic causes, including promotions and reassignments of personnel, or because of task completion (Keyton, 1993). If and when the team has completed most or all of its work, it reviews its processes and products, which are usually shared with an audience external to the team itself and whose response, in turn, is then shared with the team. Although some teams meet regularly to discuss their process and functioning (Toseland & Rivas, 1984), others do so only during the ending stage. During the ending stage team members help evaluate the process and progress of the team and may participate in an outcome evaluation. (See Chapter 10 for a further consideration of evaluation in task groups.) Team-ending program media include evaluative discussions, written evaluations, and simulations (Henry, 1992).

Because teams often end for positive reasons and with a sense of accomplishment, in teamwork there is usually less of the emotional dynamism that often affects the ending stage of treatment groups (Rose, 1989). Furthermore, during the ending stage many teams experience less of the emotional dynamics that are usually characteristic of the beginning stage. Team members should be informed about the decision to terminate or end and be involved in termination decisions related to both substantive and symbolic issues (Keyton, 1993).

CONCLUSION

Teams operate as small task groups in social service organizations that sponsor them, establish a climate and provide a context for their functioning, and contribute to assessing their effectiveness. Teams represent the collaboration of individuals to promote the interests of clients and representative agencies. Much teamwork is interdisciplinary. Although several types of teams exist and team functioning is influenced by field of practice, teams share many common characteristics, including the importance of communication and rewards for team functioning and the dynamics related to the developmental stages of the team, including the involvement and participation that characterize many teams. Team leaders tend to stress dynamics of cooperation and to manage competition among team members in order to produce results that transcend the contributions and interests of each individual member. The more conflictual the team, the more effort should go into team building. In the next chapter, some of the themes that have been discussed in regard to teams, including communication and stages of development, will be considered for task groups in general.

Chapter 5

THE PRACTITIONER'S RESPONSIBILITIES FOR THE FUNCTIONING OF TASK GROUPS

The present chapter is concerned with explicating the dynamics of the task group, the practitioner's role in the task group as the latter develops through stages, and the strategies and functions of the group that the practitioner finds of use. Although the roles performed by practitioners within task groups include those of leader, staff, and member, in this chapter the leader and staff roles will be emphasized. The leader of the task group is likely to be the practitioner, an appointed or elected member, or a volunteer who calls and conducts the meeting and implements the usual functions attributed to a group leader.

Staff refers to "a person who as part of his or her formal job responsibility is assigned to carry an executive function within a working group" (Ephross & Vassil, 1988, p. 10). In the staff role the practitioner supports and aids the appointed, volunteer, or elected leader in carrying out her or his tasks. The leader or chairperson and the staff are viewed as sharing leadership responsibilities.

TASK GROUP DYNAMICS

It is important that the leader and/or staff member possess basic knowledge about the functioning and development of task groups, including group dynamics, which are the unique forces generated by people interacting together in social systems. Four forces of major concern for understanding task groups are communication, cohesion, control, and culture.

Communication

In task groups, communication consists of both verbal and nonverbal processes by which persons influence each other and that result in social interaction within the group. Every group develops both a structure and a process for communicating. The structure involves an agreement among members, often only partly verbalized, concerning the channels and manner of communicating. The process is the complex system of interpersonal communications that conveys messages to others and consists of sending information, attitudes, feelings, and other messages that are then received and interpreted by the recipients (Festinger, 1978; Ruesch & Bateson, 1951). Northen (1969) observed, "As members of a group exchange feelings and thoughts, there is a reciprocal and cyclical influence of members on each other" (p. 17). Either consciously or unconsciously, the transmitter of a message intends to influence the receiver who, in turn, perceives both the overt and covert meaning and responds to the message. The clarity of the message sent, received, and responded to depends on the skills and accuracy of the senders and the receivers in terms of perception and interpretation.

A primary concern of practitioners is to establish an open communications system in which each member has the right to be heard. The interactions in the group can be either detrimental or beneficial in accomplishing the purposes of the group. It is the practitioner's responsibility to promote communication patterns that positively influence the process and to intervene in communication patterns that negatively affect the process. Particular areas of concern are the clarity of the communication sent, distortions in perception of one or more receivers, subgroups, status and power, physical arrangement of the group, and the patterns of interaction.

The use of feedback is an important way of checking the clarity of communication originally transmitted as well as an excellent means of testing the receivers' perceptions. By repeating the message that they heard or by asking another member to tell what that person heard, the staff are able to clarify the message intended. "When feedback is used correctly and frequently, it can prevent many distortions that arise from faulty encoding, transmission, or decoding of messages" (Toseland & Rivas, 1984, p. 59).

Subgroups, which evolve from interplay among members, are very likely to develop in task groups and usually reflect a commonality of interests of the members within them. The smallest subgroup is a dyad. Larger subgroups that may evolve include a number of triads, dyads, and isolates. The assessment of subgroups is based on positive influence in helping the task group move toward its goals. Although subgroups are capable of facilitating goal attainment, they may sometimes create barriers to goal attainment in multiple ways and over an extended period of time. The practitioner who is aware of this may decide to intervene. A common manner of intervening in such situations is by helping to change structure within the subgroup. One way is to appoint the more dominant member to accomplish a small task, such as information gathering for the next meeting, that is expected to move the group toward accomplishing its larger task. In this case the other members of the subgroup may restructure themselves, either joining the member who was appointed to the special task or ejecting the member who has left. Other means of dissolving the subgroup in task groups include appointing each member of the subgroup to a different subcommittee, structuring the meeting so that the members must cooperate with the total group in order to achieve success for that meeting, and using a decision-making process that necessitates functioning as individuals.

Initially, the members' status and power in the task group are determined by factors such as their reputation and prestige in the community, their position in the sponsoring agency, and even their physical attributes. As the task group develops, a status hierarchy evolves on the basis of the members' evaluations of each other. The criteria used by members to rank-order each other in the task group are based on their own aspirations, the ability of members to help move the group toward its goals, and other member attributes.

Status and power are important elements in the communication process within the task group, and communications tend to be directed toward the higher status members by the others (Cartwright & Zander, 1960; Cohen, 1958; Collins & Guetzkow, 1964; Smith, 1978). Members with higher status are free to talk with everyone in the group; lower status members, because of their concern about further rejection by those in the positions of power, are often reluctant to talk with the higher status persons (Kelley, 1951). The practitioner's role in alleviating this situation is to provide opportunity and expectation that every member will participate. The development of a group culture will set the scene for open sharing and communication and will be discussed later in the chapter.

The physical setting and arrangements in the meeting room influence the communication process, the expectations of the members, their perception of the prestige that they are accorded as members of the task group, and their desire to participate. Task groups may meet in a wide variety of settings ranging from an executive board room to a small cluttered room in a storefront building of a low-income neighborhood.

A common structural approach to assessing communication in task groups is to observe the communication networks among the members. In most task groups the ideal pattern for communication is either the Y or the wheel pattern because of the centrality of leadership (Toseland & Rivas, 1994). However, even with such patterns the members most distant from the leader are less satisfied than are those in the middle or the most central position. The practitioner can alter communication networks by using cues and reinforcement, by inviting participation from specific members, and by culture setting in the beginning of the group.

From these major dynamics and many other more subtle ones, an interactional pattern emerges within the task group. A practitioner may observe the same sets of behaviors repeatedly occurring in the task group, thereby developing a pattern of relating. Even the format or the way the time is spent may take on a pattern particular to that group. Over time certainly some changes will take place, but in general basic patterns will remain.

Cohesion

Cohesion or attraction between the members and the task group is another dynamic that practitioners assess and influence. In many task groups the strongest attraction to participate is related to either the tasks that the group expects to accomplish or the expected outcomes that will result. If the aims of the group and those of the potential member coincide, the individual is more likely to join and remain in the group. The attractiveness of the group is basically dependent on the needs of the members that it serves. If their needs are met they remain and bonds develop; if not, they may leave the group (Merton, 1957; Northen, 1969).

Over time, as members interact with each other, affective ties develop and cohesion increases. In addition, if members are allowed to participate fully as they become more involved, they become more committed to the tasks and purpose of the group. Cohesiveness is important because of the many ways in which it affects the functioning of the group. Sage, Olmsted, and Atlesk (1955) found that attendance was better and there were fewer dropouts in cohesive groups. Some other advantages of cohesive groups are that people feel free to disagree and even to express hostility (Pepitone & Reichling, 1955), make more attempts to reach agreement (Back, 1951), and tend to work harder regardless of supervision (D'Augelli, 1973; Landers & Crum, 1971; Martens & Peterson, 1971). As interaction and communications occur and relationships develop, communication is promoted with the results of the interaction depending on the competence of the practitioner.

Control

Some forms of social control must be in place for task groups to remain together and to function. Because the achievements of the group are dependent on interacting and working together, some consensus must exist regarding the agreed-on tasks and the parameters of acceptable behavior. Hare (1976) identified three levels of social control: formal control, by the rules and regulations imposed by a large organization; informal control, through the social pressure of small intimate groups; and self-control, which occurs in an initial social act when the individual modifies his or her behavior in anticipation of the response of the other person or persons.

Norms are an important element of social control that provide a standard of behavior expected from the others in the task group. Although overt norms tend to be clearly identified verbally, covert norms may be equally applicable. There may be an expectation that members raise their hands to be called on to speak or that once the meeting has begun no one is to leave the room.

When members join the task group, each brings his or her own values and norms. Over time, with interaction among the members and with the rules imposed from outside the group, a set of group norms comes into being. In general, group norms remain throughout the life of the group; however, sometimes the members may find reasons to modify them. The evolution of norms results from the total process. As people interact they are influenced by more subtle forces such as the status and roles of the person speaking or holding a specific view of a situation.

Culture

As the task group initially comes together, members attempt to determine whether others have purposes and goals similar to their own and if this particular system of individuals will meet their needs. Hare (1976) indicated that "the shared expectations developed in the current group are added to the prior ones as group members go through the process of culture building" (p. 19).

According to *Webster's Tenth New Collegiate Dictionary* (1992), culture is "the integrated pattern of human knowledge, belief, and behavior ..." (p. 282). Culture develops from the values and norms of each person, the expectations and rules imposed from outside the task group, the influences caused by member roles and status, and the mutual experiences of group members. In order to support and develop the dynamic forces of the group, a system of norms is essential. Practitioners can aid this development of group culture by assisting in establishing and clarifying norms as the group begins.

STAGES OF TASK GROUP DEVELOPMENT

In addition to assessing and intervening in the major dynamics of the task group, the staff helps the group move through its developmental stages. During the stages of development noticeable changes occur in the behavior of members and the functioning of the group. (See Chapter 4 for a consideration of the developmental stages of teams.)

Many models of group development have been identified, and commonalties between them have been noted (Northen, 1988; Toseland & Rivas, 1984). Models that identify three stages (beginning, middle, and ending) are often used. "The rationale for a three-stage model is that there is greater agreement on the issues to be addressed at the beginning and ending of a group than there is in intermediate stages" (Northen, 1988, p. 176). This rationale is applicable to task groups in which the purposes vary among them, which results in the middle stage being diverse in structure, content, and process.

Practitioner's Role in the Beginning Stage

At first the individuals come together as a collective. As some of the initial dynamics described take place, the task group evolves. The content and process that occur in the group are influenced by the values and beliefs of the practitioner. The description of work with groups in this chapter is based on the professional values of social work. As the task group begins, the staff are simultaneously focused on the tasks to be accomplished and on the social-emotional level. Certainly, work in task groups requires practitioner behaviors at both levels. While focusing on tasks, the practitioner gives some consideration to group maintenance, and vice versa. However, for the sake of clarity, the practitioner roles will be described as task or maintenance focused, depending on the prevalence of behaviors in each area.

When the task group first comes together, some clearly identifiable tasks must be initiated. Some of the practitioner's early concerns are the informal introduction of individuals to each other before the group session begins and the subsequent scheduling of this process as a part of the formal agenda. In general, when task group members introduce themselves, it will be in terms of who they are in relation to the problem of concern. For example, a group formed to have transportation services extended to a particular community might describe how their lives or the lives of others of concern are affected by this lack of current services.

Such commonalities in concerns help members realize that others are interested in many of the same issues. Often an individual believes that he or she cannot influence the situation of concern, but in joining with others, he or she sees that there is hope. The practitioner can be helpful in this process by assisting members in becoming more aware of their common interest. This can be accomplished by making brief summary statements after a member has introduced him- or herself, such as, "Joe, you, like Sally and John, are interested in attaining bus services so your clients can reach health care services." After introductions, another way of focusing is to ask members specifically what issues they have in common, thus allowing them to discover or at least become aware of their similar concerns.

A second important task in the first session is for the staff to state clearly the purpose and function of the task group. "Members who uniformly understand the group's purposes and goals develop a common direction for their efforts" (Zander, 1982, p. 4). Members may have already been informed of the group's purpose and function in the initial interview, if one was held. However, even if all the members have been told previously, it is still important to discuss it with the other members present in order to clarify for each person that all are there for the same purpose. Within limits, it also allows members an opportunity to make changes in structure and function to better fit their expectations. It may also suggest to them that they have the power to influence the content and process in the group. To enhance this latter purpose, it is important that the staff provide as much flexibility as possible in areas such as the time and place of the sessions and allow for discussion and negotiation.

Another area of influence or feedback in task groups is the expectation that members contribute items for the agenda of the meeting. Often this allows members to participate directly in the content to be discussed in the current session or in a future session. Sometimes the practitioner may ask members in the session to add any item for the agenda for that day or invite them to submit items for a future time.

A third task to be accomplished in the beginning stage of the task group is to set goals. In some instances, major group goals have already been determined by the agency or organization requesting a committee or other task group. Often, in addition, there are specific group and individual goals that must be identified and discussed. After the purpose of the group has been agreed on, members begin to specify goals that will help to attain these aims. In most instances, after a few group goals have been ferreted out by discussion, individuals are able to see how their goals coincide or support those of the total system. Often, individuals in a task group may be focused on gathering information or on completing some other assignment that is related to providing necessary resources. For example, an agency committee attempted to improve relationships between its major client group, teenagers, and the local police department. Mr. Bloomer, a group member, makes a verbal contract that he will find out the police policies in regard to stopping and searching juveniles. More specifically, he will interview the chief of police and attempt to get the procedures in writing. Both group and individual goals should be stated very clearly so that evaluation of achievement can be more readily assessed. (See Chapter 10 for a discussion of methods for evaluating process and outcome.)

In addition to the task focus, the other level of focus is the social-emotional or group maintenance one. In the beginning stage, many of the staff's task behaviors are laden with social-emotional content. Even the informal introductions in the beginning of the first session are intended to develop affective ties between the members and to begin to establish a culture. The practitioner, through his or her activities, can model some of the content and behaviors expected from the group members.

As members introduce themselves and commonalities are determined, task concerns are established, and the discovery of similarities between members helps to develop affective ties. As indicated earlier, cohesion is primarily dependent on the purpose of the task group; however, the evolution of a group that can work cooperatively and effectively is also dependent on the social-emotional connections that are made.

The practitioner's statement of the purpose of the task group is also intended to establish social-emotional connections. It helps to promote trust by the staff and a level of comfort within which members can participate, and it models honesty and trust as an expectation for member participation.

Encouraging members to participate in discussion of the purpose and goals and to contribute agenda items to the task group demonstrates that each member is important to the group and has the potential to influence its functioning. Validating the worth and dignity of each person creates an atmosphere in which member satisfaction in problem solving is established.

In addition, practitioners attempt to be aware of the thoughts, feelings, and experiences of the members. Becoming part of the task group is exciting for some members but creates anxiety for others. Initially, as individuals come to the meeting, they question what the mission or the charge to the group is, how it will be accomplished, and where they will fit within this process. Often, participation is hesitant and reluctant. A variety of ideas may be introduced, but there may be little willingness to discuss any of them. Most members seek to be accepted by others and attempt to present themselves in the most favorable light.

During the beginning stage, members attempt to determine their relative power and competence. Often, most of the discussion is directed to the leader, and little risk taking occurs. Over time, as members become more comfortable with each other, a few people will begin to try out their ideas. Others observe in order to determine what happens to risk takers. When they find out that verbalizing their ideas is accepted and often valued, then they too begin to participate more freely. As members discover that they will not be rejected because of their ideas, cohesion increases and the group becomes ready to move into the next stage, which is more directly focused on the mission of the group.The practitioner must also intervene in this interpersonal process using both task and group maintenance behaviors in order to help the members move through this stage and develop a readiness to move on to the next stage.

Practitioner's Role in the Middle Stage

During the middle stage the task group is self-governing and operates in an autonomous manner in which change is acceptable. The ideal middle stage of a task group should be a democratic microcosm in which there exist "a balance and continuity between legitimated authority, operating within established channels, on the one hand, and spontaneous expressiveness and creative change, on the other" (Ephross & Vassil, 1987, p. 19). When the group is able to function in this manner, the members participate in decision making, moving toward task accomplishment and regulating the group maintenance processes, especially in conflict resolution.

The middle stage is based on the accomplishments of the beginning stage. The task group has developed structures such as norms, subgroups, communication patterns, and status, which will help the group resolve the issues of power and control. Members have tested themselves and others in regard to limits in content and process of the group and are ready to take over the power and responsibility for conducting the group. The practitioner is expected to serve as a resource for the work to be done. There may be some alteration of subgroup membership as there are subtle shifts from an emphasis on social-emotional behaviors to an emphasis on task behaviors. Subgroups often are formed in the beginning around commonalities in personal characteristics, social interests, and other social-emotional factors. As the members become more comfortable with each other and with the leader and/or staff member, these issues become less important. Now the focus becomes accomplishing the purpose of the group, and individuals may move from their initial subgroups to ones that are based on a common area related to the work to be done. As these changes occur, the members dare to share differences without being rejected, act in cooperative ways, discuss alternatives, and make decisions.

Conflicts often occur during the middle stage and are either worked through or accommodated by the task group. Accommodation may take the form of developing majority and minority opinions in regard to any of the three areas of problems, plans, or solutions. (See Chapter 6 for consideration of the minority position in task groups.) Committees within the same group may work on differing areas of the same problems, thereby accommodating differences.

The role of the practitioner during this middle stage is to help the group exert the effort essential to accomplish the desired outcomes. Often during this stage, the group and members are experiencing cycles of success and productivity that may add to their motivation to participate and accomplish the tasks. In the early part of the middle stage the staff is likely to actively model desirable behaviors by organizing and encouraging members to become more involved. Then, as this is accomplished and the group takes more of the power and responsibility, the practitioner often assists as required.

Group maintenance by the practitioner during the middle stage is focused on attempting to help the group eliminate barriers for task group progress. (See Chapter 6 for a consideration of how to handle problematic behaviors.) Another common problem in groups is that hidden agendas may also require understanding and intervention at the social-emotional level. The practitioner sanctions members' equitable participation, namely, "the level of participation that is in keeping with the individual's information, knowledge, or other contribution to the group's efforts" (Huber, 1980, p. 185).

During the middle stage, most of the work is focused on the objectives that have been identified earlier in the life of the task group. After the group has formed and has become cohesive and members have gained some trust of others and have found a comfortable position within it, relatively little energy is required to maintain the group as a unit. Consequently, most of the interaction is related to solving problems and producing a product.

Practitioner's Role in the Ending Stage

Although the ending process in task groups has received little attention in the literature (Toseland & Rivas, 1984), experience suggests that the group often ends when the product or problem solution has been attained. A formal or informal evaluation verifying the accomplishments of the task group contributes to the satisfaction of its members.

Task groups (along with treatment groups) have evaluation processes and rites or celebrations of accomplishment. The emphasis of evaluation in task groups is almost entirely related to the product and to those persons viewed as having made important contributions to that final outcome. Therefore, evaluations primarily deal with the accomplishment of the task and results, rather than members' contributions to group maintenance. Along with this informal evaluation may go a celebration of having completed an important but difficult task. Members may feel a real sense of accomplishment and satisfaction.

What happens to the group cohesion that has developed? Because the group purpose has been completed, one might assume that the major attraction to the group no longer exists. Certainly, during the time the group has been meeting, interpersonal attraction has developed within the group. When the group ends, these relationships often are carried over into the community outside, between coworkers in an agency or volunteers in another setting or into other areas of life.

STRATEGIES AND FUNCTIONS
FOR THE PRACTITIONER'S USE

Three major strategies that practitioners utilize in working with a task group are the use of time, agendas, and group minutes. In regard to time, the total development of the task group is patterned and somewhat predict-able. Each session, too, is cyclical in nature. In dividing a task group session into three segments, the most predominant type of behavior shifts as the group moves through the session (Bales, 1952; Bales & Strodtbeck, 1951). In the first time segment, the members are collecting information; in the second time segment, they are evaluating; and in the third time segment, they are pressing for decisions or resolutions.

Such information about the natural process for the use of time in task groups can be utilized in the preparation of an agenda for a session. The agenda items to be attended to in the first segment of the meeting are "start-up" concerns, the next period is a "heavy work period," and the final one is a "decompression period" (Tropman & Morningstar, 1985, p. 39). A process similar to that of the development of the total group occurs in each session. In the beginning the members are engaged in the process, then there is a period of intense work, and finally there is preparation for ending. This inclination toward patterned functioning should be taken into account in constructing an agenda.

Tropman and Morningstar (1985) have suggested that agenda items be divided into three batches: One includes informational items; the second, decisions that must be made; the last, items for discussion. Items are sorted items in this way so that when they are placed on the agenda, a note can be made next to each, identifying the action that is to be taken. The agenda includes a series of subjects and, next to each, an indication of expected action as follows: for discussion, for information, or for a decision. After culling the items to be included in that specific session, they are arranged in the designated order.

The minutes of the task group are expected to closely reflect the agenda of that session. Although there are differing points of view regarding the content of this document, a very clear, succinct method should be used that follows the agenda items exactly. The agenda is used in the minutes with relevant discussion and decisions noted next to each item (Tropman & Morningstar, 1985).

Although much of the work of the practitioner is accomplished in the group sessions, there are many tasks and functions that must be completed before the next meeting. The focus is to follow up on tasks taken on by members or committees and to make sure that members are prepared to participate in the most effective and efficient way for the next session. This may require making phone calls, working with subcommittees, coordinat-ing work between subgroups, and contacting other resources. The practi-tioner also maintains contact with the administrators, other staff, boards of directors, and other significant groups in the community.

The practitioner must see that the minutes and reports are prepared for the next session. In some cases these are gathered and sent out along with the agenda to members before the session. The preparation of the agenda requires that the staff request and receive topics to be included, that the topics be culled to determine whether they are appropriate, that specific items be selected for use, and that the relative order in the total list is determined. The last step is to mail the agenda and any relevant material to the members.

CONCLUSION

This chapter has described the roles and major concerns for the practitioner in working with task groups. Tasks and social-emotional behaviors of the staff and members have been identified in relation to group dynamics, group development, work in each session, and work between the sessions.

In establishing the task group, major tasks to be accomplished include focusing the group on an agreed-on purpose, implementing group goals, and establishing a group from a collection of individuals. Promoting an attraction to the task group through the development of affective ties, culture building, norm setting, modeling, and reinforcing are important to prepare the group to move into problem-solving activities.

This chapter has focused on some of the broad functions and structures in working with task groups. The following chapter identifies some of the problematic behaviors that are frequently manifested in task groups and suggests some strategies for working with them.

Chapter 6

HANDLING PROBLEMATIC BEHAVIORS OF THE TASK GROUP, SUBGROUPS, AND MEMBERS

Problematic behaviors that interfere with the functioning of task groups command the attention of leaders and members and should be recognized, understood, and handled. (See Chapter 4 for a discussion of difficulties commonly experienced by teams.) Included in this chapter are methods of working with problematic behaviors, such as monopolization, aggression, and other dysfunctions, that are exhibited by individuals and that pose problems for the group. (For a consideration of intergroup problems see Thalhofer, 1993.) Problematic behaviors experienced in the task group transcend the individual level and involve problem behaviors of subgroups and the whole task group. They include hidden agendas, groupthink, risky shifts, and conflicts.

Five assumptions underlie the consideration of problematic behaviors in the social services task group. One assumption is that leadership of task groups is exercised to increase the members' awareness of and motivation toward working cooperatively to achieve the purposes of the task group. A second set of assumptions is that conflict is inherent to task groups and that the effective leader resolves conflicts constructively. A third assumption, which is related to social loafing, is that the composition of many task groups is such that although they contain members who function adequately in meeting the purposes of the group, they also are likely to have one or more members who are functioning inadequately in meeting the purposes of the group. A fourth assumption is that task groups function more effectively when difficulties that commonly arise in their functioning are handled by leaders and members who possess and utilize appropriate knowledge, attitudes, and skills consistent with working together on common goals. A fifth assumption is that although highly cohesive task groups often function well, hazards to their effective functioning accompany very high levels of cohesiveness.

AGENDAS

Agenda has two meanings, one relating to the overall purpose of the group, and the other more customary meaning referring to the specific plan for a given task group meeting. In most well-organized task groups, explicit agendas for meetings serve the function of publicly structuring and communicating the central topics for deliberation. Explicit agendas are generally prepared by leaders with input of the group members and are subsequently distributed in advance of the task group meeting. Explicit agendas help the task group meet the demands of accountability by providing a specific set of items that can be readily checked to see that the work of the group is indeed accomplished.

Although explicit agendas tend to be ubiquitous, task groups sometimes function without them. For example, at one agency a committee often met without an agenda. Consequently, meetings evolved with little sense of purpose or activity. Most of the discussions were social and emotional in nature, and members, although feeling chummy with those in the group, had little sense of accomplishment.

In addition to explicit agendas, many task groups have one or more hidden agendas that are concealed by some members and obscure to other members. Although all task group members are cognizant of and discuss explicit agendas at the beginning and at other points during the group meeting, hidden agendas are those that a person or subgroup is aware of and discusses privately, often between regular meetings of the task group. Covert or secretive interests lead one person or subgroup to manipulate task group process and seek power through a hidden agenda. An example of a hidden agenda in a task group is the pursuit of self-interest by one or more members of the group. For instance, in a task group devoted to providing social services for refugees, members of one ethnic group surreptitiously attempted to have resources shifted to programs that they felt adequately represented their interests as well as those of the agency clients.

Although task groups sometimes have one type of agenda, they commonly possess both types. Explicit agendas are more professionally acceptable than are hidden agendas. Hidden agendas tend to divert attention from and at times may be in conflict with explicit agendas, thereby impeding the effectiveness of the task group in achieving its purposes. Hidden agendas are sometimes products of the external affiliations of task group members. Furthermore, in some task groups a social dilemma occurs in which the self-interested activities of individuals combine in a potentially disastrous manner for the task group itself (Messick & Brewer, 1983). For instance, the explicit agenda of a regional planning and coordinating council for child abuse prevention services was to promote interagency cooperation. However, a hidden agenda of one subgroup was to assume a preeminent, dominant position. At least in part because of the actions of the subgroup, the council was unable to effectively promote interagency cooperation.

CONFLICTS

Location of Conflicts

Conflicts occur within and among members, subgroups, entire task groups, and organizations (Putnam, 1986). Differences of opinion and professional judgment rendered in one task group at times conflict with those rendered in another task group, with some such conflicts revolving around underlying issues of professional turf and domain. For example, in one task group subgroups developed in the form of cliques that became engaged in conflict with one another over power. The result was that voting on key organizational issues tended to reflect the views of the clique rather than those of the individual member.

Sources of Conflict

Conflict has multiple sources and may be viewed from multiple perspectives (Putnam, 1986). Task groups with considerable internal competition tend to be conflictual as members contend with one another for scarce resources. Sources of conflict in task groups include processes of judgment and evaluation (Scheidel, 1986). The emotional dynamics related to conflict include withdrawal, defensiveness, barriers to communication, hostility, and retaliation. Also, task group members with differing values, ideologies, and backgrounds often have different opinions, perspectives, and worldviews that come into conflict within the task group (Putnam, 1986). Unfortunately, antagonisms of race, ethnicity, religion, national and regional background, gender, and age tend to linger under the surface of some task group discussions. For instance, a social service agency devoted to education, training, and research activities to support practice was confounded by the discord among group members who expressed considerable difficulty in understanding and appreciating each other's perspectives on the many tasks they faced.

Conflict: Functional and Dysfunctional

Conflict is viewed as either functional or dysfunctional, or both, depending on when it occurs (Deutsch, 1969). Inevitably, most task groups experience conflict, although conflict-free interaction will occur at some time periods in many task groups. From a functional perspective, conflict is part of a Hegelian dialectical process (Churchman, 1971) that represents opposing perspectives that are resolved through a transcending synthesis. Such conflict often occurs between the group majority and the group minority and results in a reciprocal change of each party's opinions and judgments (Moscovici & Mugny, 1983).

Conflict is an inherent aspect of sound decision making that emerges when a task group considers and weighs a range of divergent alternatives and in doing so develops splits that become conflictual (Putnam, 1986). Conflict can improve the quality of task group decisions, because high-quality alternatives may be generated during the course of the group discussion (Coser, 1956).

The view of conflict as dysfunctional is prevalent at least in part because conflict tends to evoke anxiety (Putnam, 1986). However, despite the lack of desirability of anxiety as an emotion, it is usually useful in motivating members to resolve conflict. The perspective of conflict as dysfunctional is that it is inherently destructive and should be avoided. Although avoidance is certainly one way of dealing with conflict, that is a limited strategy, and if used exclusively in some situations it actually may be hazardous and result in an escalation of conflict.

A task group composed of members who believe that conflict is dysfunctional is likely to attempt to avoid conflict. Consequently, groupthink develops, and the cohesive task group is ineffective in its ability to make decisions. Conflict about a decision is functional prior to the acceptance of a decision, but it is dysfunctional and destructive after the decision has been adopted by the group as a whole (Putnam, 1986).

Types of Conflict

Discordant and dissonant communications, disagreements, and differences of opinion are manifestations of conflict that are often expressed in task groups. At an extreme, conflict is represented as overt animosity. Conflict, which may appear at all stages of group development, tends to be more pronounced during one phase than in the other, relatively nonconflictual phases.

Conflict may be of several types, including latent conflicts, which are often subtle, and manifest conflicts, which are overtly expressed. Under conditions in which the task group is highly stressed, latent conflicts become manifest. For instance, a small family social service agency was under considerable stress because of legal charges brought against its executive director. The agency staff, which functioned as a task group, had considerable latent conflict that became manifest in the course of a staff meeting as members confronted one another in an insulting fashion on the same day that the additional stressor of the news of a funding difficulty was announced.

Another type of conflict includes interdisciplinary conflicts, which reflect rivalry between professions, a common feature of the group dynamics underlying teamwork (see Chapter 4). Conflicts of interest (also called mixed-motive tasks), which tend to be present in interdisciplinary conflicts, are the subject of legal and ethical interest and are commonly experienced within and between task group members. An example of a conflict of interest is that of a member of a task group with a vested interest being put in a role that is ostensibly neutral or impartial. A coworker was asked to provide an evaluation of a colleague and was unable to do so because of the personal nature of their relationship.

Interpersonal conflicts, which are often present in task groups, are related to personality conflicts (Rohrbaugh, 1988). Although some persons in task groups tend to be engaged regularly in interpersonal conflicts, with engagement in conflict reflecting personal styles of members, other members of task groups avoid interpersonal conflict. For instance, in the interaction of a task group at an inpatient mental health unit, one member, who tended to be verbose, regularly engaged other members in conflict, as if for the sport of it. However, some of the other members refused to be drawn into such interaction. Consequently, the progression of conflict was less than if they had been drawn into the interaction.

Cognitive Conflicts

Cognitive differences among persons include the varied ways that people process information, and they underlie many interpersonal conflicts. Indeed, cognitive conflicts may be viewed as a type of interpersonal conflict related to inconsistencies in judgments among persons that tend to be exacerbated by task characteristics (Brehmer, 1976). Cognitive conflicts, which are often unrecognized, are often mistakenly identified and labeled as conflicts of interest, yet they are more subtle and difficult to resolve than conflicts of interest. For instance, in a task group designed to assist a treatment team with difficult diagnostic decisions, some members tended to develop their diagnoses using a subjectively oriented clinical approach, whereas others tended to use a more objectively oriented, actuarial, or empirical data research-based approach.

Cognitive and Outcome Feedback

Task group members can use cognitive feedback to offer reasons for having different positions, explain each other's viewpoints, and improve a judgment process. Cognitive feedback includes the relative importance that individuals attach to each piece of information they have and the form of the functional relationship between such information and the judgments of the individuals. For example, in a social services task group that was oriented to make many decisions about policies in the organization, the members often gave the reasons why they held views about particular issues and explained the importance of the information on which they based their views.

In contrast to cognitive feedback, outcome feedback provides feedback at one point in time to individuals about the correctness of their judgment regarding a particular situation or case that was under consideration earlier. For instance, a policy-oriented task group regularly received reports about the accuracy of individual members' predictions about the outcome of program interventions.

Some evidence exists that cognitive feedback is superior to outcome feedback in improving the accuracy in judgment of individuals and reducing interpersonal disagreements (Hammond, Stewart, Brehmer, & Steinmann, 1975). For example, for many years a prominent child welfare agency conducted a task group to supervise its workers. At first the group used outcome feedback. However, during the past 2 years the new supervisor who led the group emphasized cognitive feedback and discussed with the staff members how they made placement decisions. Several of the members commented that they felt that the atmosphere was more congenial in the group now that their discussions emphasized how they thought about the decisional aspects of the placement process. They reported less interpersonal conflict in the supervisory group now than they had earlier when the previous supervisor focused on the end point or outcome of the placement process. Furthermore, agency records suggested greater accuracy of decision making and improved performance, reflecting learning and its generalization, that occurred recently for members in the supervisory group run using a cognitive feedback approach.

Conflict Management

Task group leaders often view conflict as inevitable in the task group setting and use a combination of approaches to manage it. In hierarchical decision-making task groups in which members disagree about means to ends, the problem is made explicit, and group methods are useful in reaching agreement (Vroom & Yetton, 1973). Such methods of managing group conflict include having the group recognize the problem as one affecting the entire group and asking members to contribute to controlling or even eliminating conflict. For instance, at a task group meeting the leader brought up the problem of morale and defined it as a group problem to be solved. The staff members present commented on several members who missed the meeting, and several acknowledged that having members miss meetings was indeed a problem. After a few minutes, one of the members talked generally about disagreements and conflicts occurring in organizations. Then, a few members commented to each other that such observations were applicable to the present agency as well. After overhearing the comments, the leader brought them to the attention of the whole group and the members pondered them for a while. Then the members discussed supporting one another in various ways at work.

The leader is able to use many additional techniques to manage conflict. Microleadership processes of definition, direction, and structuring are also useful in working through conflict (Scheidel, 1986). Adhering to administrative procedures and following explicit agendas are useful means of handling conflicts. For instance, at the highly conflictual meeting of a task group, the level of conflict was restrained by the task group leader's returning the discussion to the agenda and resuming with a noncontroversial item.

According to Putnam and Jones (1982), conflict can be managed through nonconfrontation, that is, smoothing over the conflict; solution orientation, or use of compromise; and control, or forceful confrontation. Putnam (1986) and Crouch and Yetton (1987) have described numerous effective skills and techniques of conflict management that are used by leaders to facilitate group discussions in task groups in which conflict is prevalent, as follows: The leader decides which conflicts are to be attended to and prioritizes the order of attending to conflicts. Leaders often decide to handle conflicts that are more easily resolved before handling more difficult ones. Also, some leaders wish to concentrate on central conflicts before attending to peripheral conflicts that may be insignificant or may diminish without added attention.

Listening to the viewpoints expressed by parties to conflict is a vital management skill that can be developed further by task group leaders who are primarily accustomed to expressing their own points of view. Promoting communication includes encouraging conflicting parties to assertively express their viewpoints. The ability to be receptive to and use others' points of view is also important in resolving conflict. Because many conflicts represent a lack of understanding and are compounded when each side becomes entrenched in its own viewpoint, furthering understanding is a worthy objective. Role-play procedures are useful means for members to gain an appreciation of opposing points of view, thereby defusing conflict within task groups. For instance, at a contract negotiation session between representatives of a social services union and board members, an impasse was reached. The mediator asked each side to select one member to role-play a representative of the other side. The social services union representative was more willing to enact such a role than the board member, who initially muttered how ridiculous role playing was in a negotiation session. When the two persons role-played, they caricatured the other side. Subsequently, each side complained to the mediator that the other misrepresented their own point of view. Despite the conflict that ensued after the role play, the representatives on each side nevertheless began negotiating again, and some progress was made in resolving the disputes.

The use of people, including experts, from outside the task group can be helpful in resolving internal differences of opinion among members. At times, the conflicting parties may look to the outside persons to mediate the disagreement or even to proclaim that their cause is just and their side is right. For instance, at a meeting of a social service unit attached to a court setting, considerable disagreement reigned about the point at which inter-vention services ought to be given and who the client was. The unit leader decided to bring in an outside expert who engaged the task group in a discussion that eventually led the members to try, within the constraints of the court setting, for early intervention and for a broader definition of the client than was currently the purview of the service unit.

Thoughtful analysis is important. Uncovering and validating underlying assumptions to arguments usually result in progress toward conflict reso-lution. In general, the consequences are that parties to conflicts are able to recognize the basis for their disagreements. Recognizing the potential areas for agreement is useful, too. As in most situations, some areas of agreement usually exist between conflicting parties in task groups, so that noting any common ground between opposing viewpoints tends to promote softening and closeness of positions as well as a rapprochement leading to further, perhaps unanticipated agreements. For instance, at a seminar sponsored by an educationally oriented social services task group, two powerful and influential members became embroiled in a vituperative argument about accountability that centered on differences in strongly held beliefs and philosophies about the role of the social service agency. The intervention of a third and ostensibly neutral person who was also a powerful and influential individual served to defuse the conflict and allowed the seminar task group to continue its activities.

Negotiation is a key skill that involves arbitrating and mediating be-tween opposing parties in order to bring them to a position that both are willing and able to accept. However, when the leader perceives that the parties to an intense conflict have locked-in positions, postponing a con-frontation is sometimes useful because the confrontation may be less intense and more manageable at a later date, after the parties have become less emotional. For instance, at a homeless shelter a conflict had developed between two members that interfered with the performance of their work duties. A leader of an interagency task group on homelessness was called in to deal with the conflict. The leader was concerned that the meeting would be confrontational. Therefore, the leader scheduled the meeting involving the two members for a time when additional neutral parties, who would be likely to provide a calming effect, would be present.

Integrative styles of conflict management by leaders, in which conflict resolution benefits both parties equally, tend to be most satisfying to the parties to the conflict and most satisfactory for the task group (Wall & Nolan, 1986). For example, a task group was immersed in a conflict over the issue of appointing representatives to a national social service commission.

The task group leader was able to obtain a compromise in which both parties agreed on a representative who was sympathetic to but not directly representing either side. The members were visibly relieved, and the atmosphere in the group was much improved, so that the group was again able to focus on its task activities.

Although task group leaders are often chosen because they possess conflict resolution skills, in some cases the leaders require training in leading discussions with task groups that are in conflict. Such leaders may further develop their conflict resolution skills through a leadership training program. Furthermore, task groups must be ready to deal with their own conflicts, which in turn requires them to choose members with conflict resolution abilities, to make conflict resolution skill training available, or even to consider replacing those members who cannot acquire the given skills with others who are more willing and able to become more skillful.

SOCIAL LOAFING

When feelings of anonymity and deindividuation occur in task groups, a drop in motivation ensues (Latane, Williams, & Harkins, 1979; Mullen & Baumeister, 1987). Responsibility becomes diffused when some members of task groups do not work as hard as the other members (and not as hard as they might as individuals not in a group setting). Furthermore, those individual members of task groups make less of an effort when working collectively (in which their inputs are combined into a united group product or score) than when working individually or coactively (in which case their inputs are not combined) on the same task (Karau & Williams, 1993).

When the task group is evaluated and rewarded on the basis of the entire group's performance, irrespective of the actual level of individual effort, some individuals believe that it is rational for them to free ride, although the combined effect of many members doing so is likely to lead to a dramatic reduction in the performance of the task group (Kerr, 1985).

Social loafing usually breeds resentment within the task group. Some members who expend a great deal of effort are aware of and uncomfortable about how much effort they are expending in comparison with others who are expending little effort. Harder working members may perceive the effort differential as a shirking of responsibility by less hardworking members. Members who expend a great deal of effort tend to feel that they should receive a greater reward for their effort than members whom they perceive to be loafing; if they are not rewarded, the hardworking members believe that an injustice has occurred. Hardworking members generally wish to encourage or even coerce further work or activity by less active members. In extreme situations, hardworking members may even desire to punish the members who have engaged in social loafing through means such as administrative actions or sanctions. For example, in a child welfare agency, members of a task group were writing a report to a funding agency on the implementation of an innovative program. Although most of the members were hardworking and productive, it appeared to them that one member was loafing. Indeed, the resentment tended to build so much that the loafer was scapegoated and joked about by the other members.

Nonloafing task group members can perceive social loafing as an undesirable phenomenon that has a negative association with productivity and effectiveness. Leaders of task groups should be aware of its prevalence. A useful approach to demonstrating and controlling social loafing is to establish procedures to measure and evaluate the contribution of each member of the task group, thereby making all efforts public and comparable (Harkins & Szymanski, 1987). Monitoring and publicizing individual performance and providing feedback to members about their performance as well as that of their subgroup are likely to contribute to controlling social loafing (Karau & Williams, 1993). Increasing the meaningfulness and uniqueness of tasks assigned to individuals and conveying the importance of the contribution of each individual to accomplishing the task are also useful means of reducing social loafing, as are increasing the creativity of the task, promoting personal involvement in working on the task, and directly increasing the efforts of others in the task group through pairing procedures (Brickner, Harkins, & Ostrom, 1986; Jackson & Harkins, 1985). While doing so, one must also be moderate in drawing attention to individual members because extremes of attention to individuals are also likely to lead to performance decrements known as social impairment (Mullen & Baumeister, 1987). For instance, at the annual dinner of a task group supporting a social agency, staff members who had agreed to play the piano and flute had received so much attention that their performance suffered.

To prevent the occurrence of social loafing, it is desirable to select members who are interested in contributing to achieving the purposes of the task group (Swap & Associates, 1984). Some research indicates that women and persons from Eastern cultures, although still likely to loaf, tend to do so less than men and persons from Western cultures (Karau & Williams, 1993).

Furthermore, increasing the cohesiveness of the task group (Williams, 1981), including setting a positive tone during group meetings and recognizing and rewarding the contributions of all members, is a useful way of increasing the motivation of the group members. Inevitably, setting consequences for the efforts of all group members is likely to have expected as well as unexpected impacts on social loafing. Given the necessity of avoiding punishments in order to maintain the morale of the task group, it may be necessary to reassign individuals who are not contributing adequately to the group.

POLARIZATION AND DEPOLARIZATION

Task groups are subject to both polarization, that is, movement to a more extreme or less moderate position, and depolarization, or movement to a less extreme or more moderate position (Shaw, 1981). In a related manner, task groups may make risky and cautious shifts, with the former receiving more attention. Apparently, risky shifts are related to at least three sets of social processes, including diffusion of responsibility, persuasive arguments, and social comparison. Members in task groups tend to experience a diffusion of responsibility (as occurs in social loafing), which contributes to the risky shift phenomenon. When diffusion of responsibility occurs, task group members feel absolved of any personal or individual responsibility for the decision or action of the task group. Consequently, they are likely to make riskier choices than under circumstances in which they are individually held responsible.

A related process, that of persuasive arguments, indicates that after being exposed to and listening to the views of others in task groups, individuals make riskier choices. For example, after participating in a financial seminar, the director of a professional organization, in consort with a task group entrusted with the retirement funds of the social service practitioners in its employ, decided to move a substantial portion of its investments out of relatively safe yet low-yielding money market funds and into more aggressive growth and income funds. A third process, that of social comparison, suggests that societal admiration for and valuing of risk taking influence individual members of task groups to support riskier choices.

Furthermore, individual members of a task group compare their own views with that of the group. If the group encourages more risk, they tend to move in that direction. For instance, a task group was considering the adoption of a novel social intervention that was proposed as a help in promoting the rehabilitation of the elderly persons who visited their day center. When the more conservative members of the group saw that the other members tended to take a chance with the new intervention, they too went along and agreed to give it a try.

DEINDIVIDUATION

Because of the effects of social influence, people often behave more impersonally in a task group than in a dyad. Although some of this behavior is desirable, a problematic aspect exists because in some task groups members act in a deindividuated or dehumanized way that is less rational or moral than the way they might act in a dyadic situation (Swap & Associates, 1984). Deindividuation is a process in which a group majority focuses on and behaves inconsiderately toward a group minority (Mullen & Baumeister, 1987). Some but not all the individuals in the group are able to contribute their own opinions and perspectives. For instance, at a juvenile justice facility a staff meeting was held to discuss the performance of the executive. The majority did not allow the minority to express their opinions during the meeting, which made it difficult to obtain a valid picture of the staff's level of confidence in the executive.

Apparently, although some individuals maintain their integrity in task groups, others lose themselves and change their interaction patterns within groups. Through a process of deindividuation, task group members experience and sometimes enjoy a temporary escape from the constraints of their selves, including their customary ways of behaving.

The process of deindividuation affects persons who are members of social services task groups as well. In contrast to those who are individuated, task group members who are deindividuated have less involvement in self-processes—including attention, monitoring, regulation, and control—and more involvement in group processes. In highly cohesive task groups, deindividuated members tend to lose touch with their own moral codes and personal values and are more likely to function according to group norms than on the basis of their own individual values. Although sometimes group and individual norms are equivalent, a discrepancy often occurs that should be resolved. In highly cohesive task groups, the discrepancy may be resolved in favor of the group norms. If such norms are prosocial and professional, little difficulty exists. However, highly cohesive groups tend to lose control and allow irrational behavior. Indeed, it is difficult for a task group composed of deindividuated members to engage in rational decision-making processes.

Therefore, it is the charge of the task group leader to counteract tendencies to deindividuation that occur in the task group. The effective task group leader monitors levels of cohesiveness so that they are maintained at appropriate intermediate levels. The leader takes action to decrease cohesiveness if it is at such a high level that rational discourse cannot readily take place within the task group, and takes action to increase cohesiveness if it is at such a low level that the group cannot interact and maintain itself with the unity required for cooperation within the task group. Such actions include modifying (decreasing or increasing) pressures toward conformity, unanimity, and consensus. For instance, statements encouraging free expression of ideas tend to decrease pressure in the task group. To preclude deindividuation, the task group should be structured so that all members participate and present their own views. Members should be encouraged to express differences of opinion and minority opinions.

GROUPTHINK

Social Pressures

Task groups are settings in which social pressure can be and is applied to influence individual members. For example, a task group in a social services consulting organization was faced with an administrative decision. The leader was good friends with one of the members of the task group and decided to use their friendship to encourage the members to vote in accordance with the views and interests of the leader.

Such social pressures include attempts for the group to reach unanimous decisions. For example, a task group appeared to be united in regard to a funding decision. However, A, who was a crucial member appointed to be in charge of the decision, opposed it. B, a powerful person who was actually several administrative levels above A, spoke to A in an attempt to have A vote with the others in favor of the proposal. (See Chapter 8 for extensive consideration of decision making.)

Decision Making

Groupthink is a phenomenon that explains some of the actions of small decision-making groups (Hensley & Griffin, 1986). Groupthink is a pattern of thinking by group members in which social desirability supersedes rational analysis. In task groups, social influence processes often work to either promote or avert errors in group decision making (Hirokawa & Scheerhorn, 1986).

When groupthink occurs, decision making is likely to be ineffective (Janis, 1982). Group discussions are limited in regard to the scope of alternatives that the group considers. For example, a task group operating under a groupthink pattern organized to provide day care services for working parents considers only church-related auspices and does not consider nonsectarian possibilities, thereby limiting itself in regard to the scope of objectives considered.

Groupthink is characterized by the group's lack of consideration of obstacles to the implementation of a decision. Under groupthink the group fails to consider the means to the desired ends. The overbearing and unjustified confidence of the group in its ability to weigh alternatives and make decisions results in its neglect of a wide range of alternatives and its inability to fully use the decision-making process. For instance, a substance abuse agency with a very good reputation was overly confident about its ability to be reaccredited and was therefore surprised when it had considerable difficulty in meeting the revised standards of the accrediting body.

Groupthink poses a difficult problem because task groups often make decisions with consequences that have a significant impact on persons outside the immediate task group. As a result of groupthink, task groups may leave relatively unexamined the often considerable risks or potential negative consequences associated with their decision. For example, a task group devoted to planning was composed of political appointees by a state executive. The consequence of the task group's misallocating the provision of mental health services because of its groupthink process was inadequate assistance for some clients, until the political process resulted in a correction.

Unanimity

Pressures toward consensus and unanimity are commonly manifested in task groups. When such pressures are evident, members whose minority views are inconsistent with those of the majority may modify their views in response to the majority view. Pressures toward unanimity represent an interest in avoiding conflict and maintaining morale. Such pressures also reflect an interest in maintaining a high level of cohesiveness, particularly when the extragroup environment is viewed as hostile by group members. Pressures toward unanimity are manifested as the desire that the task group speak in one voice, despite the fact that rarely, if ever, does this represent the views of the members.

Groupthink presents a hazard in highly cohesive groups. Pressures toward unanimity, which are manifest in groupthink, are of concern because such pressures toward reaching consensus override the potential contribution of individual members, stifle dissent, miss one or more steps of the decision-making process, and lead to decisions of poor quality that are neither well thought out nor well considered and that are likely to be destructive to persons inside or outside the task group (Swap & Associates, 1984). Consequences of pressures toward unanimity are prevalent when the very existence of the task group and its ability to reach its goals are in question and the task group is likely to be reaching for quick solutions to its problems. During such times, the leader must be particularly careful to work against group processes that are intolerant of diverse and minority views.

Characteristics

In social service task groups that compete with others for scarce resources, groupthink is manifested in three sets of characteristics (Janis, 1982). One, members overestimate the group, falsely believing in their invulnerability as members of the group and assuming that their motives and actions are principled, just, and moral. For instance, as a result of a groupthink phenomenon a task group decided on a series of placement policies that would severely restrict the types of cases served by the agencies under its jurisdiction.

Two, members are close-minded, use rationalization, view opponents as evil, and underestimate them as weak. For example, a task group under intense financial pressures began viewing a competing service provider as corrupt, immoral, lazy, and incompetent and was surprised when the other agency received the grant for the development of services in the same geographical area.

Three, the task group experiences pressures toward uniformity. Members (A, B, C) who disagree with a stated view are subject to pressure to conform by other group members (D, E, F) who function to protect the remaining members (G, H, I) of the group from information that may upset the equanimity of the group. Despite doubts expressed by one or a few members (A, B, C), all members (A . . . I) censor any doubts they experience in order to present a false image of group unanimity to themselves and to others.

Uniformity

Uniformity serves at least four functions, including that of allowing the task group to operate in an efficient manner as it attempts to reach its goals (Swap & Associates, 1984). However, at a certain point the drive to efficiency is counterproductive, so that the cost exceeds benefits. For example, in a social agency a hard-driving executive secured approval for a proposal and provided little time for discussion among the participants. Although the proposal was approved, considerable bitterness ensued, interpersonal relations were strained, and further activity in the task group did not proceed smoothly.

A second function of uniformity is group maintenance. In many environments, uniform groups maintain themselves well. When relatively few differences of opinion are expressed by members, there seems to be little interpersonal friction to disturb the harmony and tranquillity of the group. However, in other environments, uniformity is not the norm, so major differences of opinion are expressed. Although this can be effective, major differences can also lead to difficulties in group maintenance.

A third function of uniformity is the maintenance of the task group's relation to the external environment, which is often strong when uniformity is high. By appearing unanimous to others, groups that are high in uniformity appear to be impervious to criticism or challenge from outside and are in a powerful position. In contrast, highly heterogeneous groups may have a dual relationship to the external environment, including some support and some opposition.

A fourth function of uniformity is the provision of a relatively simple set of self-evaluation standards for the task group. As such, uniformity promotes simplicity, which is easier to handle in the evaluation context than is complexity. In contrast, highly heterogeneous groups tend to have more complex approaches to developing standards for self-evaluation.

Three sets of factors contribute to the development of groupthink in task groups. First, although many task groups are cohesive, those in which members become excessively uniform in their thought patterns are likely to develop a groupthink pattern. Second, the presence of structural faults in the group, including buffers that prevent the group from obtaining information and opinions from outside the group, subjective leadership patterns, haphazard procedures, and similarity between members in social background and beliefs, tends to increase the probability of the occurrence of groupthink (Janis, 1982). A task group that consists of members who have the same upbringing and values will be limited by the perspective the members take of a given problem under consideration by the task group. Task groups are information-processing systems, and groupthink is problematic in that it affects the ability of the group to properly process information. Groupthink is characterized by an inadequate search for information and is associated with distortions in processing information that reflect the subjective views of the members. Third, groups are stressful for members. Stress is primarily an individual-level phenomenon that may be experienced by many individuals in the group. Groupthink tends to occur when the group is subject to stress (Hensley & Griffin, 1986).

Prevention

Five sets of activities are useful in preventing, postponing, and reducing groupthink. One, as mentioned earlier, is reducing excessively high levels of cohesiveness and uniformity. Two, given that the size of a unanimous group appears to be directly related to conformity (Swap & Associates, 1984), reducing group size is likely to reduce the tendency to develop groupthink. Three, bringing in persons from outside the task group to give their views and opinions can also counteract the groupthink phenomenon. Four, modifying leadership style to reduce pressures toward conformity can be effective in reducing groupthink. Five, engaging in a formal decision-making process, including emphasizing the rational aspects of examining advantages and disadvantages of each decision option, tends to lessen groupthink.

PROBLEMATIC MEMBER BEHAVIOR
IN THE TASK GROUP

Problematic behavior, such as excessive off-task interaction that interferes with processes leading to the desired outcomes of the task group, is a frequent occurrence in task groups. Although some social-emotional interaction serves the function of releasing tension in the task group, dysfunctional effects are produced when such interaction becomes excessive. Although sometimes relating to the topic under consideration, private discussions in task group meetings that disrupt the attention processes of other members are problematic. Personal needs of members for socialization can disrupt the group process unless they are handled by the group leader. When a noticeable amount of off-task behavior is present, the effective leader attends to it and encourages the members to be involved and participate in the group in an appropriate, on-task manner. For instance, in one task group the leader was irritated at the continuous murmuring and lack of attention by some of the members. The leader called attention to the task at hand, thus involving the members and eliminating the distracting activity.

Unequal participation rates are common occurrences in task groups. In some instances a member will monopolize group discussion. This difficulty is usually handled by establishing group norms about how long any one member can speak or by taking turns. For instance, in a task group two members became known for their monologues and distracting, although amusing, bantering. Consequently, other members became listless and group interaction became off task. In this instance, the leader was able to limit the monopolization by warmly and humorously engaging the two members and acknowledging the value of their contributions but firmly moving the group ahead.

When the actions of the minority members conflict with the views of the majority, the former tend to be perceived as problematic by the latter. However, through a consistent presentation of its positions, the group minority has the potential to increase the originality of group discourse and even to convert the majority to its positions (Moscovici & Mugny, 1983).

Members of the task group who represent a minority position are subject to harassment and intimidation by majority members who disagree with the former's stated positions, leanings, values, or beliefs. If and when such conflictual interaction occurs, the leader restrains the more aggressive members of the task group and protects those who are harassed and intimidated or otherwise engages in a conflict resolution strategy described previously. For instance, one of the members of a social services task group freely expressed her opinions, which were listened to yet ridiculed by other group members. At one point, another member began heckling the member and had to be restrained because the damaging statements exceeded the group norm for criticism of another member.

Task group members may have personal problems or may suffer from mental disorders that are disruptive to the group process (Dore, 1993). The leader might discuss such situations with a supervisor or mental health or organizational consultant in order to find a way to reduce the impact of such problems on the group. The leader of the task group models how the other members can handle such members with respect and appropriate control. For example, in one task group a member with a paranoid personality disorder distorted the information available to the members and believed that others were engaged in a conspiracy against the member. The uproar created was such that the member was referred for mental health treatment.

CONCLUSION

Task groups are often confronted with problems at the group, subgroup, and individual levels that affect their functioning. Such problems include individual instability, hidden agendas, social loafing, polarization, deindividuation, groupthink, and conflict. Leaders and members of task groups should recognize such problems and deal with them quickly and effectively to ensure the stable functioning of social service task groups. Although social influence is a potent force in creating and maintaining deindividuation and groupthink, it also can be used to overcome the problems confronting task groups.

In the present chapter, the focus has been on problems in functioning that tend to beset task groups. The following chapter describes the types of problems that social service task groups are often called on to solve, as well as the process groups typically use to generate solutions.

Part III

PROBLEM-SOLVING TECHNIQUES

Chapter 7

THE PROBLEM-SOLVING PROCESS

Problem solving occupies much of the time in task groups. A problem represents a concern or a difficulty that is experienced and identified by one or more members of a task group. Problems vary in their levels of concreteness and abstraction. Problems also vary in regard to how much controversy they generate, as when issues become contentious and conflictual. Although many problems dealt with by task groups have solutions, some represent dilemmas or difficulties that the group believes are irresolvable at the point they are considered. The present chapter will consider what it takes to improve problem solving by discussing the kinds of problems addressed by social service task groups and by considering the problem-solving process as a series of steps.

THE TASK GROUP AS A SITE
FOR PROBLEM SOLVING

Many task groups are formed to deal with problems that have come to the attention of social service organizations and require the attention of the task group. For example, a leader of a tenants rights organization was apprised of specific housing conditions that were inadequate. The leader referred these to a citizens advisory group in order to obtain advice on how to proceed.

Task groups in social service organizations are often faced with resource limitations as they seek the solution to problems faced by clients. For example, a task group in a social welfare agency was faced with the agency's problem of trying to meet an increasing demand for material social services, including reimbursement for food for poor families. The agency's budget was inadequate to meet all requests. In attempting problem solution, the task group subsequently tried to increase resources and meet client demand.

For many years small groups have been used as means of solving problems (see Chapter 1). The development of ways to improve problem solving in task groups draws considerably from the ideas of John Dewey (1933), the originator of pragmatism, who developed a systematic method for solving problems (Somers, 1976). Many of Dewey's ideas were used as the basis for the development of the scientific method. The problem-solving approach that Dewey developed was adopted in many fields, including education, business, and the social services.

In addition to being formed to demonstrate their effectiveness in problem solutions, task groups, like the social service organizations of which they are a part, demonstrate to a public body that they are dealing with problems in ways that represent the interests of multiple constituencies, including service providers, client populations, and community interests. Through their composition, problem identification, analysis, and solutions, task groups demonstrate to the task group leaders and members, as well as to other persons and task groups in an array of social service organizations, that they are representative and democratic. By legitimizing the problem-solving process, task groups generate support for implementation of proposed solutions to problems.

TYPES OF PROBLEMS ADDRESSED

Most task groups consider themselves to be primarily oriented to problem solving. Such task groups may be in agencies that are beset by a range of difficulties. External problems are those that they hear about—difficulties experienced outside the organization, for example, those involving community relations.

Some of the social and organizational problems that come to the attention of and often frequently experienced directly by task groups in social service agencies are recurrent or chronic and require continual attention, including the implementation of partial solutions on an ongoing basis. For example, a task group in an agency providing social services for adolescents and their families had an enduring communication problem in that the group did not regularly receive financial reports from the agency executive.

In contrast to chronic problems, acute problems tend to be unexpected. If they are major ones, they can threaten the equilibrium of the task group and even the wider organizational environment. For instance, at a social service department in a large state hospital setting, one of the members of the task group had committed suicide, leaving a note indicating a feeling of ineffectualness in helping clients. The repercussions were dramatic, leading to a morale crisis among members of the group that spread to others in the hospital. The social service department head organized an interdepartmental task force that developed means of recognizing the achievements of staff in working with clients.

Timing is an important consideration that affects problems addressed by task groups. As a leadership variable, timing is related to effective problem solving by task groups (Maier & Sashkin, 1971). Indeed, some evidence suggests that task groups with leaders who delay mentioning their preference for a particular way of solving a problem may be better at problem solving than task groups whose leaders mention their choice at the beginning of discussion about choices (Anderson & Balzer, 1991). Having members pool their knowledge and viewpoints is often helpful in developing high-quality choices in regard to feasibility and adoptability.

Social service task groups deal with a wide array of problems, including the ones described below, separately or simultaneously. Those problems related to the functioning of a social service organization include concrete or material problems as well as human problems. For example, a task group met to discuss and ameliorate the problem of heating and cooling the large physical plant of the building housing the agency. Apparently, the heating and cooling system had become antiquated, and it had to be dealt with because its malfunctioning was occurring in a sporadic manner that interfered with the delivery of services to clients.

Some organizational problems dealt with in task groups have an impact on the survival of the social service organization. For instance, a small social agency that had been founded as an alternative type of agency discovered that it no longer had the mandate, funding, and clientele to continue operating as it did in earlier years. A task force was formed to deal with these problems. Plans for a reconstituted agency that was somewhat more conservative were put in place, although some staff ultimately resisted the change.

Group-level problems, which are discussed within task groups, sometimes repeat organizational problems. For instance, cohesion of the organization may be represented in the cohesiveness of constituent task groups and subproblems of turnover.

Client problems are frequently discussed by task groups. Given that social service organizations require clients for their operations, ensuring an adequate flow and supply of clients is of concern in many social service agencies. For example, in one setting the client supply and the related demand for services were cyclical. During certain time periods the agency was barely able to cope with demands for its services, although during other time periods the agency was overstaffed. This problem was brought up in a task group meeting.

Once clients have entered the social service agency, processing them through the system is of concern to task groups (Hasenfeld & English, 1974). For instance, a timing problem arose in a social service agency that handled job unemployment claims because the processing unit received the claims from the intake unit late. This resulted in a delay in claim processing and decreased client dissatisfaction.

In some social service settings, social control of clients is a problem addressed by task groups. For instance, at a correctional setting that had experienced a number of violent attacks by inmates against service providers, a task group met to discuss the problem of worker job safety.

Disruption of organizational functioning by clients is also considered in task groups, especially in corrections, health, and education. For instance, security was a concern at a correctional setting with a number of attempted outbreaks. Another example is that of a client who infiltrated the computer files of a social service agency and changed agency information. That problem was discussed in terms of computer security, law enforcement, and treatment considerations.

Health problems of staff and clients are often the subject of task group deliberations, especially in settings in which persons are at high risk for illness and disability. For instance, at a day care center for children, a task group discussed the feasibility of having day care providers receive flu shots. The pros and cons were discussed.

Administrative and management problems are of concern to many staff groups. For instance, at one agency, there was a system of management by objectives that a labor committee of social service providers actually found somewhat cumbersome. A joint labor-management committee discussed the creation of a management system that would be agreeable to all parties.

Fiscal and budgetary problems of an agency and their impact on programs and individuals are frequently deliberated on by task groups. For example, a budget committee of a large mental health center met to deal with ways of coping with proposed cutbacks in funding and to consider ways of developing alternative funding sources.

Task groups also deal with leadership problems. For instance, a task group within a welfare rights organization addressed the following problem: Many members thought that the leadership was not dramatic in placing its demands before state officials. A committee was created to see what should be done about the problem.

Policy problems present in the larger environment, including that of the national headquarters of state and local social service organizations, are also dealt with by many task groups. For instance, a task group that had been formed to revise the bylaws of a state family service organization debated whether to include material that had been requested from a group of concerned parents.

Legal issues are often discussed in task groups. These are sometimes referred to attorneys who are in the group. The family of a patient who had died at a mental retardation facility sued the medical director and several staff members, claiming that they had been negligent in the care of the patient. The issue, widely discussed at the facility in an informal manner, was also dealt with in an executive committee that engaged the facility's legal counsel in regard to representation and defense issues.

Ethical problems are also handled by task groups whose responsibility may be to monitor professional behavior (Reamer, 1990). For instance, an ethics committee of a large health and social services complex considered the problem of service providers who were referring their clients to their private practices.

Some problems receive attention because of the sponsorship and philosophy of the agency. For instance, a task group of a secular social service agency discussed the morality underlying the provision of social services to a wide range of populations, including criminals, delinquents, and substance abusers. At one task group meeting, some of the service providers said they believed that they would find it difficult to work with clients who persisted in immoral actions.

Religious problems are also the subject of task group work in social agencies. For instance, at a large correctional center, some inmates complained that the food served was in violation of their religious practices, and they requested a dietary change. A task group at the center, none of whose members shared the faith of the inmates voicing the complaint, attempted to respond to the problem in a way that considered budgetary guidelines, policy directives about treatment of inmates, and the risk of legal action.

Humanitarian problems are discussed in task groups in many agencies. For instance, the policy group of a large international child welfare organization was faced with issues of trying to maintain its budget and its organizational viability despite increasing numbers of children who were coming to the attention of the agency.

Intra- and interorganizational political problems and related conflicts over power, turf, and authority surface in many task group deliberations. For instance, a political action committee affiliated with a national professional social service association discussed whether to support a candidate for public office. The candidate was a member of a political party whose positions tended to oppose the interests of the association.

Professional problems, including relationships among the helping professions, are considered for task group deliberation, too. For example, an executive committee composed of the heads of the disciplines of a multidisciplinary child guidance clinic discussed interdisciplinary problems concerning who was in authority in interprofessional collaborative work with clients.

Accreditation problems are regularly considered by social agencies that seek approval from regulatory bodies. For instance, a task force on accreditation of a facility that wished to have its accreditation status renewed considered problems relating to what was considered appropriate use of social service interns according to accreditation standards.

Supervisory problems that are not resolved within meetings between supervisors and their subordinates or that represent transcendent issues are handled in group meetings. For instance, an agency review committee determined supervision to be idiosyncratic, depending largely on the wishes of the supervisor. The committee attempted to deal with the problem by developing standards for supervision to guide all supervisory activities at the agency.

Although personnel problems are appropriately dealt with in personnel committees, they receive attention at other meetings as well. Performance problems are also the subject of task group work in the social services. For instance, one social service research organization discussed the problem of one candidate who had been given hiring preference but was not performing as well as other staff members of the organization.

Problems related to multiple aspects of evaluation, including policies, implementation, and impact, are also considered by task groups. (See Chapter 10 for a discussion of evaluation methods in social service task groups.) For example, a group of social service providers challenged a task group to develop culturally sensitive evaluation procedures that reflected norms and values of a minority culture.

Morale problems, especially pervasive ones, are widely discussed in group meetings, in a covert way as well as occasionally in an overt manner. For instance, one agency that had been beleaguered by a series of other problems related to lack of support from the external environment met to consider ways of improving morale within the agency.

Hiring problems, including difficulties in finding appropriate candidates, are dealt with by administrative task groups and personnel committees. For instance, a recruitment committee had the problem of having an insufficient number of applicants for the agency's openings and determined that the problem related to the unfavorable image of the agency.

Given that the social service context is usually characterized by much interaction between people, inevitably interpersonal problems emerge. One set of problems concerns the development of hostile relationships, aggression, and violence within the work setting. For instance, a task group was faced with trying to find a way for two senior staff members who were very emotionally involved in an antagonistic relationship to work together on a project of vital importance to the task group and to the agency.

Another set of interpersonal problems concerns the development of romantic relationships within the work setting. For example, in one agency the director and a junior staff member became romantically involved, causing problems concerning the remainder of the staff's sense of being treated equitably. The problem was alluded to indirectly during staff meetings. Because it was not discussed publicly, explicitly, and thoroughly, it remained a source of difficulty to the task group. Consequently, the couple resolved the problem by relocating. However, the agency was then faced with the additional problem of recruiting two new capable persons.

Problems related to promotion of staff members, including qualifications, standards, and political considerations, are also widely discussed in and out of meetings. For instance, at one state agency a task group met to discuss and approve the promotion of a staff member but had to consider the problem that the agency had placed a freeze on promotions for the year. The task group discussed the policy issues involved and appointed a representative to the administrative advisory group of the group in which the impact of the freeze was discussed.

Caseload burdens are also considered, especially in regard to their direct relationship to work stress experienced by staff members. For instance, at a child welfare agency, task group problems of burnout were considered to be tied into problems of excessive caseload and insufficient support.

Retention and turnover problems are also the subject of task group work and are often the focus of policy and program change. For instance, a discussion of agencywide problems at one social service agency indicated concern about how frequently staff were leaving the agency, resulting in many inexperienced persons unfamiliar with agency procedures and interventions being left to handle client demands.

Loss of personnel is considered by task groups and is of particular concern in agencies that have a difficult time recruiting and retaining staff because of factors such as location, salary, and benefit structures. For instance, at a small agency one senior and two junior staff members resigned at about the same time. The agency's executive committee met to discuss steps to improve the salary and benefits of staff members.

STEPS OF THE PROBLEM-SOLVING PROCESS

The problem-solving process in task groups consists of a series of steps that, although analytically distinct, tend to flow into one another in their implementation (Compton & Galaway, 1984). In terms of both logic and procedure, the steps of the sequence are interrelated and involve preceding and succeeding steps (D. A. Garvin, 1993).

The first step of the problem-solving process, problem identification, is crucial because a problem must be defined by the task group before steps can be taken to resolve it (Maier, 1963). A problem can be identified by the task group in several ways, including the transmittal of information and communication from internal or external sources. Ordinarily, a problem must reach a certain threshold in order to be perceived as a problem. For example, an internal problem experienced by the task group itself, namely, the lack of an articulated purpose to the task group, was finally vocalized by one of the more articulate members of the group.

The nature of the task group, and in particular the leader's style, will determine the extent to which problem identification stems from the members or stems from the leader. Usually, although members identify problems for discussion, the leader of the task group is the person who is most responsible for identifying problems for group discussion and for deciding when a particular problem is to be discussed. In task groups with nondirective leadership styles, the members are more likely to identify problems. In task groups with more directive leadership styles, the leaders themselves are more likely to be those who actually identify the problems.

After the problem is identified, task group members and leaders should develop their understanding of the problem. The second step of the process, then, is that the identified problem is clarified through discussion that makes parameters, limits, boundaries, and situational features apparent (Toseland & Rivas, 1984). For instance, the leader of a task group composed of two professional subgroups at a family service agency was called on to deal with problems in the delivery of home health and social services. The nurses and the social workers requested and received explanations about problems primarily related to the expertise of each other's profession.

Often, only one problem is discussed at a time when the task group enters the problem-solving phase. Nevertheless, discussions frequently focus on the interrelationship between a particular problem and other related problems. For instance, a task group at a social agency was considering a problem pertaining to suspected sexual coercion of clients. The discussion next focused on related issues about education of agency clients in regard to their rights, responsibilities, protections, and means of addressing grievances and complaints. The discussion then turned to one way of dealing with the problem. Other more direct remedies to the problem of suspected sexual coercion of clients were considered as well.

Following the group's clarification of the nature of the problem, the third step is that proposed solutions, which may have been voiced in an informal manner in prior deliberations of the task group, are now actively and formally considered, voiced, and discussed as options for dealing with the problem. Although occasionally a task group will consider only one solution, ordinarily multiple solutions are considered (C. Garvin, 1987). Furthermore, the task group leader usually encourages consideration of more than one possible solution. For instance, a task group concerned with the problem of team functioning within the agency considered options of improving interdisciplinary training opportunities, encouraging team members to attend interdisciplinary conferences, and reconstituting several key task groups to reflect the interdisciplinary nature of the agency staff.

Lasting solutions to major problems sometime require major changes, such as restructuring and redesign of the mission and functions of the agency, which are sometimes unattainable goals. However, immediate and partial problem resolution that is satisfactory to those who are concerned about the problem is at times a readily attainable goal.

After the task group has considered its options, the fourth step is that each option is debated in terms of its advantages and disadvantages.

Depending on the nature of the task group, this step is enacted at any one of a number of levels of formality. In some groups, each option is formally identified and written up on a medium such as a chalkboard that all members can see. In other groups the options are discussed in a freer and more interactive manner.

After discussing the relative merits of each option, in the fifth step the task group members express their opinions about the feasibility of adopting particular options that are available to them through voting and arriving at a prioritization of potential solutions. The democratic character of the task group is expressed through voting. There are various ways to define what is considered an acceptable solution to the task group, including obtaining a majority of the votes. (For further discussion of decisions and decision rules, see Chapter 8.)

Deliberating on the group's views about solving the problem and reviewing the results of the voting precede arriving at an agreement about a solution to be implemented. Ordinarily, the voting process culminates in the sixth step, namely, the task group's acceptance of either a simple or complex solution.

After the task group agrees on a solution, the seventh step is initiating the actions required to implement the solution. In some social service organizations, the task group that analyzes the problem and recommends a solution may actually be the unit that is responsible for accepting the solution and even for implementing it. In other cases, the seventh step may involve making recommendations for implementing the solution to other parties or groups. For instance, a task group monitoring the organizational performance of a series of group homes for adolescents in a geographical region uncovered the problem of inadequate documentation of intervention activities at one of its sites. The solution arrived at by the task group was to implement a monitoring procedure involving conferences and direct participation of staff at the site. The task group delegated the solution to a state group and instructed the state group to report back to the regional office of the organization for adolescent group homes.

The task group usually prepares a written report that includes, in either extended or summary format, an analysis of and recommendations for problem solution and solution implementation. Then the report is forwarded to another person, such as an agency executive, or another task group, such as a committee, at which point it is accepted as is, modified before implementation, or rejected and probably referred back to the task group. Further directives are then made for the implementation of a solution.

Eighth, the success of the implementation of the solution in addressing and resolving the problem is evaluated by the task group itself and by others, given that in some social service organizations the evaluation task is the responsibility of another unit, such as another task group. For the most part, when the task group that proposed the problem solution conducts an evaluation of its own effectiveness, it is simpler and easier to close the circle in the problem-solving process than when the evaluation is conducted by an outside body.

The evaluation of task group problem solving occurs at two levels: the political, symbolic, public relations level and the actual, tangible, substantive level. Furthermore, evaluation occurs at several time intervals, including the immediate and the longer term success of problem-solving efforts. For political and public relations purposes, the perception of attempted and actual problem solution is of vital administrative concern. Improving perception of solving a problem, which reflects an actual interest in solving the stated problem, in itself may solve the problem faced by an administrator who has to please a particular constituency. For example, a task group at a child guidance clinic located in an urban area was faced with charges from community leaders that they were unresponsive to the social problems of community members. The agency director formed a joint community-agency task force to address the problem, and its problem-solving efforts were widely publicized.

The issue of problem solution is an empirical one; that is, it can be decided only on the basis of actual experience. Although the best thinking, which is based on the task group leaders' and members' knowledge and experience, is used to develop a solution, its effectiveness is tested in novel real-world situations. If the problem has been successfully solved, the problem-solving process is complete. However, in the ninth step, if insufficient success is achieved in resolving the problem at either the symbolic or actual levels, the problem returns to the attention of the task group through formal and informal channels. The ninth step demonstrates the continuous cycling-through process that is characteristic of ongoing problem solving in a social service organizational environment.

In some instances, after a considerable period of time has passed and the task group readdresses a problem, the task group has changed in its mission, objectives, and composition. For instance, a task group devoted to long-range agency planning was faced with a problem that had last been seen by a group composed of different members: the creation of a long-range plan consistent with accreditation demands. Because of the high degree of turnover at the agency, all members of the long-range planning committee had not been present at the creation of the last such plan. This created a problem in providing continuity within the agency, although new ideas and perspectives were abundant.

Although in practice task groups are likely to vary in regard to the time and attention they devote to particular steps of the process, all the steps are likely to be considered in order for effective problem solving to take place. Furthermore, although in some social service organizations the process tends to stop at the seventh step of initiating action, it should proceed further through the eighth step of evaluation and, if necessary, the ninth step of recycling in order to be complete.

In actual problem-solving practice, some task groups progress rapidly by simultaneously combining and attending to several interrelated steps in one session. Although many formally organized task groups follow the problem-solving sequence according to the steps of the model identified and described previously, task groups tend to enter the sequence at any step (Hoffman, 1979). Furthermore, if the problem-solving method is implemented as an unstructured or semistructured discussion, the group moves back and forth between steps as it gradually proceeds. For example, in a task group considering the problem of a rapid rise in the number of complaints about suspected incidents of child abuse reported, the group considered as a solution the implementation of a special call-in phone number. The task group then reconsidered the definition of the problem and came up with another alternative, the formation of a special community-wide child abuse action team.

CONCLUSION

Problems are conceptualized in regard to acuteness-chronicity and in regard to simplicity-complexity (Broome & Chen, 1992). Task groups deal with many types of linked problems (Van Gundy, 1987), including those perceived as primarily situated in or affecting the external environment, the social service organization, agency personnel, social service clients, and the task group itself. (See Chapter 6 for a discussion of internal problems in functioning of the task group and their management.)

Problem-solving activities are important to the functioning of task groups, and social service organizations regularly tend to be in a problem-solving mode. The process of problem solving is conceptualized as consisting of nine steps. Evidence exists to support the effectiveness of problem solving in task groups. In this chapter, implications are drawn for the likelihood of success in handling problems faced by such groups. Problem solving for task groups inherently involves a perceived aspect based on an actual solution. The effectiveness of problem solution in social service task groups is inevitably gauged on both aspects. Decision-making procedures are closely related to problem solving and are the subject of the following two chapters.

Chapter 8

SMALL GROUP DECISION-MAKING PROCEDURES

Task groups that are engaged in problem solving are inevitably involved in decision making, which is an integral component of the problem-solving process. In solving a problem, a task group makes one or more decisions. (See Chapter 7 for a consideration of problem solving.)

Many social service task groups, including those that are executive in nature and may be involved in policy-oriented work on behalf of the agency and the greater community, are primarily oriented to decision making. Many factors affect decision making, including the orientation of the task group to make a decision, its preparation for decision making, its motivation and willingness, its task orientation, the skills of the leader and members in decision making, and the dynamics of the group in regard to cooperation and competition. Task groups make decisions in order to function properly, to come to agreement on what course of action to proceed with, and ultimately to help develop programs that will provide social services to clients. This chapter discusses the conceptual aspects of decisions and decision making, methods and techniques of decision making, obstacles encountered in decision making, and the sequelae of decision making.

CHARACTERISTICS OF DECISIONS
AND DECISION MAKING

Decision Products

The product of the decision-making process is a tangible decision that is immediately manifest to those who have contributed to the decision-making process. In social agencies decisions stem from the activities of task groups. For instance, personnel committees are responsible for filling vacancies and deciding whom to hire for particular positions.

Decision Context

Ordinarily, task groups consider at least three factors as they come to reach a major decision (Hirokawa & Scheerhorn, 1986). First, decisions have a contextual element to them, and task groups consider situational aspects surrounding the decision. Second, given that numerous potential means are available to reach particular ends, task groups consider alternative means to achieving problem solution. A decision represents a choice among a number of alternatives or recommendations (Fisher, 1974). Third, task groups consider what might occur as a result of the implementation of a particular decision. As such, two aspects are relevant, the potential consequences of implementing each alternative and the potential consequences of a chosen solution (namely, the objectives) as the group arrives at a major decision.

Task groups provide a context in which decision making occurs. Although decision making is often characterized as a process that occurs during actual meetings of the task group, variants of this occur as well. Decisions that are made in the context of the task group are based on deliberations that are either open or closed and public or private. An example of secrecy and irregular procedures during decision making is as follows: A task group was charged with making a personnel decision at a large social agency. The group decided to meet without informing or inviting one of the key senior group members, who subsequently found out about the meeting and considered voicing a complaint about the breach of normal procedures. However, the member considered the potential consequences of such an action and, after deliberating about complaining directly to the members or to others, in the end decided to keep quiet about it, feeling overpowered by the others.

Decision Makers

Decision making in task groups represents the contributions of several parties or constituencies. Social influence factors affect the results of the decision making as well. Power accrues to decision makers because decisions often have significant consequences for one or more parties connected to the social service agency. Although how to proceed in decision making is often determined by the leader, all participants (members and leaders) are involved in the decision-making process. In addition, the task group may rely on others from outside the task group who are consulted prior to, during, or after decision making, especially to provide input to the decision-making process. Expert decision making is an acceptable form of making decisions in situations in which other members of the task group either individually or collectively do not have the requisite expertise to make the required decision. For example, a mental health center task group was faced with a difficult decision in diagnosis and brought in an outside expert to consult on the case. The opinion of the consultant was carefully considered by the team when it made its diagnostic decision.

Information-Based Decisions

To counteract the hazards of making irrational decisions, task groups attempt to make rational decisions that are based on the acquisition and systematic processing of information by the group. Some research indicates that experiences of being in control maintain task group members' cognitive alertness and energy levels to allow for information processing and decision making that is constructive and creative (Sedek, Kofta, & Tyszka, 1993). Other research indicates that experiences of being in control either have no effects or are deleterious in regard to productivity of ideas (Diehl & Stroebe, 1991). Task groups rely on information that is available to them in order to make the best possible decisions. Task groups gather information from internal (within the group) and external (outside the group) sources. Task groups often form subgroups to gather information to aid in decision making. The information available in making a decision is directly related to the prestige of the agency sponsoring the task group. Furthermore, the information varies in regard to its completeness, accuracy, and timeliness, which contribute to its usefulness for the task group. Although completeness of information is a theoretical possibility, in practical terms it is a rarity. Task groups often have to make decisions on the basis of partial and missing information. As an integral component of the decision-making process, attempts to obtain vital information are often made prior to making the relevant decision. Accuracy of information is gauged by comparing views of informants or information providers as well as comparing information with other objective sources, including research materials and public documents. For all decisions, current and recent information is valuable; for some agencies, historical data are desirable as well. For instance, one task group that was working with information about public figures in government verified and added to its information base by contacting city hall.

Decision Importance

The content of the decision is tied to the purpose of the task group and the mission of the relevant agencies. Decision importance is related primarily to the purpose of the task group and secondarily to the missions of the agencies represented by the task group. The importance and centrality of the decision are a function of its close relationship to the purpose of the task group. For instance, a child guidance and evaluation clinic met to make an important decision whether to develop a new program for single-parent families.

Decision importance is directly related to the consequences for those affected by the decision. Major decisions, in regard to importance, are those with profound effects. For instance, a nationwide philanthropic organization decided to change its thrust from raising money for fund research relating to one set of health and social issues to another set.

Issues listed on an agenda require decisions ranging from moderate to major importance. However, other decisions are minor in importance. For instance, at one committee meeting of a social service agency the task group deliberated for 20 minutes about the disposition of the soft drink machine near the entrance to the facility.

Frequently, major decisions are made on the basis of a series of several smaller decisions that are clustered together or associated with one another. For instance, after several decisions had been made to add staff to provide child sexual abuse assessment and intervention within a child protective service unit, a decision was made to upgrade the status of the program to unit status within the department of social service, which would bring to it additional organizational attention and resources. Decision trees are useful devices for conceptualizing complex problems in assessment or diagnosis in clinical practice in agency settings and are also useful for tackling organizational problems.

Decision Complexity

Many aspects of decisions and the decision-making process vary in regard to simplicity or complexity. The simplest types of decisions are those that are binary, that is, characterized by requiring a yes or no answer. For example, a task group composed of representatives from several homeless shelters decided whether it wished to form a coalition representing their interests to fund-raising bodies. Although many decisions are simple, others, such as those involving strategic problems (Cosier & Schwenk, 1990), are more complex. For instance, a task group overseeing the clinical care of a troubled adolescent with a problematic diagnosis decided how to involve the adolescent's family members in treatment.

In regard to problematic situations, decisions consist of multiple decisions of varying complexity. Furthermore, decision sequences often consist of components and aspects of varying complexity. A key to effective decision making is reducing complex decisions to a series of simpler decisions.

Decision-Making Difficulty

Decisions vary in regard to the softness and hardness attendant to their creation and usually are either pleasant and easy or unpleasant and difficult for the task group to make. Furthermore, decisions are marked by their pleasant or unpleasant consequences for those persons, groups, and agencies affected by the decision, including the task group itself. Simple decisions are relatively easy to make; complex decisions are more difficult to make. Environmental situations affecting the task group itself are likely to influence the hardness or softness of the decision. For instance, because of resource scarcity, a task group in a social service agency had to make a hard decision in terms of to which of several agencies to allocate external resources. In times of greater resource abundance this would be a soft decision.

Decision Timing

Decision making occurs within the organizational time cycle of the social agencies' task groups. Decision-making task groups concerned with social services in education usually operate on and are influenced by a school-year schedule. Also, in most agencies budgetary decision making is influenced by patterns of resource availability and consumption during the fiscal year.

Three phases in decision making exist: a pre-decision-making stage, a decision-making stage, and a post-decision-making stage. In the pre-decision-making stage, the task group becomes oriented to and prepared for making the decision. Second, the task group uses the decision-making procedures to arrive at a decision. The post-decision-making stage is one in which the decision is announced and publicized and the consequences become apparent.

Decision-Making Speed

Decisiveness, or the ability to make decisions rapidly when called for, is generally a desirable leadership quality. Another aspect of timing is the condition under which particular decisions are to be made. Although normative decisions may be made under relatively relaxed circumstances, they may also be made under highly stressful ones. Some decisions are urgent and must be made quickly, in a crisis mode; others can be and are delayed and made slowly. In some agencies, decisions are consistently made under pressure; in others, decisions are made in a more relaxed manner. The context of decision making, then, refers to the organization itself and the demands that are placed on it for framing, making, and implementing decisions. In times of organizational crisis, demands are high for the task group to make a rapid decision. The recognition of a decision to be made is fairly routine when social service organizations are functioning optimally. However, in times of organizational transition or difficulty, some urgent decisions are made as a consequence of change. For example, an administrative task group in a child welfare agency was faced with simultaneously increasing caseloads and decreasing numbers of staff and had to reach a decision quickly about action to deal with the situation. Although some task groups make decisions in a single meeting, others may deliberate for multiple meetings, in which case they may take months or even years to make a decision.

Decision Quality and Correctness

It is in the interest of task groups to use processes that will result in making decisions that are judged to be of high quality (by sources within the task group as well as external to the group) at the time the decision is made, announced, and implemented. In many situations there are likely to be several potential decisions of varying yet acceptable quality, rather than a single correct decision. In decision making, the key is often to make a decision and to leave judgment of its correctness to a later time period, because the correctness of a decision, that is, making the so-called right or wrong decision, generally is evident some time after the decision is made. Often the task group is more likely to be judged in terms of whether it made a decision than on the correctness of a decision. For instance, a large child welfare organization coping with a large amount of information decided on installing a computer network that consequently vastly improved its ability to manage client and program information. Although the task group in charge of making the decision later found it could have made a more cost-effective decision, their decision was timely and of sufficient quality to make it an acceptable and implementable one.

Decision Commitment

Although consensus groups tend to have higher levels of commitment than many other types of decision-making task groups (Schweiger, Sandberg, & Ragan, 1986), the latter, and their individual members, also tend to develop a commitment to a particular decision. Sometimes the level of decision commitment is such that they then begin to search for rational support for their choice in order to justify it. For example, a task group composed of child welfare personnel dealing with the issue of staff training considered a number of choices in regard to making a decision about who would provide the training. Early in the process of considering the choices, several members became attached to the option of hiring a consultant and searched for reasons supporting it. The members discussed the budget, the tie into a national network of consultants and trainers, and the reputation of the consultant. The enthusiasm of the members resulted in the task group's choosing the particular option of hiring the consultant.

DECISION-MAKING METHODS

Group Discussion

Decision-making methods in task groups rely on group discussion. Although some groups make their decisions entirely on the basis of discussion, others use additional, formal techniques or interventions to structure the decision-making process.

Entirely or almost entirely open discussion is a rarity in many formally organized operations. For instance, during a planning meeting of a philanthropic organization whose major institutional purpose is the collection and distribution of funds collected from the public, a junior employee proceeded to speak freely to all present about many topics that were not directly related to the task at hand. The other members of the task group were bewildered and astonished at such unprofessional behavior.

In some task groups the discussion is open and freewheeling throughout the entire process; in others, such discussion occurs only at set periods of analysis and during the development of alternatives for decision making. In other groups, discussion tends to be relatively closed, which is a characteristic of authoritarian leader decision making.

Group decision-making discussion varies in formality. Although some task groups tend to be structured in how they approach decision making and use formal discussions as ways of making decisions, other groups tend to be unstructured in their approach and in general rely extensively on informal discussions. For instance, at a small, alternative social agency operating on a shoestring budget, the staff members tended to make their decisions in a strictly informal manner by loosely discussing them together using a sociable approach, allowing considerable reign for emotion to play a part in the process.

Decision Emergence and Decision Making

Some decisions appear to emerge in task groups, often through an informal decision process in which agreement, perhaps even consensus, occurs. Other decisions are deliberately made. Decision emergence usually refers to a gradual, even natural, development of a decision consensus. Decision making refers to an active use of directive procedures that ensure that a decision is reached, often in a relatively brief time period.

Consensus Decision Making

In some task groups, especially small ones, a consensus model in which all members must agree in order for a decision to be made is useful, particularly when the task group is composed of members who are cooperative. Indeed, the decision-making process moves more quickly when the members are readily able to resolve conflicts that arise. The consensus model, which is consistent with social work values, is a highly democratic and participative one that promotes equalization of power among members, as in teamwork. Implementation of the consensus model involves open discussion and examination of the assumptions of all individuals who are party to the decision-making process. Consensus occurs when all members accept the underlying assumptions and recommendations pertaining to the decision.

The advantage of the consensus model of decision making is that it promotes input from a wide array of task group members, thereby facilitating subsequent acceptance of the decision. It is most useful in situations in which decision making is not urgent and in which input from all members is useful in contributing to the quality and the acceptability of the decision.

One disadvantage of the consensus model is the extensiveness of the time-consuming deliberations required to reach a consensus decision, thereby making it relatively inefficient to use. When it is urgent for a task group to make a decision quickly, the time-consuming nature of consensus decision making militates against its use. Another disadvantage of consensus decision making is that organizations concentrate decision-making powers in persons in certain roles or positions in the organizations and are unlikely to wish to diffuse that responsibility to people in other ranks, roles, or statuses. Furthermore, persons in social service organizations with responsibility accrue some power that goes along with decision-making ability and tend to wish to maintain that power and not necessarily share it, as a prerogative or benefit, with others. The consensus decision-making model, which tends to fully allow direct participation by all members on all decisions, is practical for use in small and more alternative social service agencies. However, many long-established, hierarchically organized social service agencies must rely on symbolic representation or voting in order to move forward on their decision-making agendas.

Voting

After deliberating on an issue, task groups frequently use a voting procedure to reach a decision. The views of the task group toward the decision outcome are reflected in the proportion used for a decision. The requirement for approval or agreement on a decision varies, with specific examples including rule by a simple majority or by a three-fifths, two-thirds, or three-fourths majority. A task group in an organization that requires a relatively high proportion of yes votes is selective, quality oriented, and, when uncertain, more likely to be inclined to make a negative decision than a positive one because of the decision consequences. The greater the proportion of yes votes required for the acceptance of a decision by the task group, the more likely that a negative decision or a disapproval will be attained and the more difficult it is to pass a measure and reach a decision. The higher the proportion of votes required for acceptance, the less likely that the decision rule will be used. For example, a three-fourths rule is rarely used. Often, majority rule is used by task groups because of simplicity of use, ease of calculation, social acceptability, and allowance for easy passage of measures. However, in some task groups the decision rule either is implicit or varies, at least in part, because of cognitive conflict. For instance, in a task group in a substance abuse treatment center in which there was considerable conflict, the task group had no consensus on what would be an acceptable decision rule, and decisions were made on a haphazard basis with those who commanded the floor managing to get decisions made and partly supported by the group.

Decisions, which represent the views of at least some of the members of the task group, are characterized as either positive or negative. A positive decision is an affirmation of a proposal. For example, a task group at a mental health agency voted in favor of a proposal to build a new downtown service unit that would provide better access to service to indigent populations. A negative decision is a rejection of a proposal. For instance, a large social service agency board turned down the request of its executive director to fund the director's proposed membership in an exclusive social club. Indeed, many of the board members viewed the request as being an outrageous one.

Following a vote, the decision is generally recorded, and deliberation continues on to the next decision. In well-functioning task groups the decision rules are explicit, such that the circumstances under which decisions are made are known to the participants of the task group.

OBSTACLES TO DECISION MAKING

The Role of Cognitive Conflict

Decision making usually encompasses some representation and resolution of conflict. Cognitive activity, which may include varying amounts of conflict, is basic to decision making. An assessment of the existence of cognitive conflict in a group setting, including quantitative (amount) and qualitative (type) aspects, is warranted. Such an assessment is taken by the task group under the direction of the leader. Furthermore, some decision-making techniques actually increase cognitive conflict (Priem & Price, 1991). (See Chapter 6 for a discussion of cognitive conflict as a problematic behavior in task groups.)

Cognitive conflict often emerges during discussions of decision options. In addition to reflecting various interests or constituencies, the results of a vote are interpretable as reflecting cognitive conflict.

Although it is frequently unrecognized, when recognized cognitive conflict provides the potential for resolution of differences in cognitive processing, style, and approach that are inherent to cognitive conflicts. For example, in a long-range planning task group for the development of mental retardation services, two members voted differently because of a difference in how they viewed the resources of the client population. After a discussion of differing ways of thinking about viewing such resources, more understanding was apparent in group discussion, and the gap between some of the members' viewpoints diminished.

Decision Delay

Although making a decision is usually a preferred option, delaying the making of a decision is yet another choice available to the task group. Often decision delay represents a response to an avoidance-avoidance conflict situation in which either decision choice has potentially undesirable consequences for those making the decision and for those who announce or publicize it. For instance, the board of directors of a family service agency was faced with a couple of unpleasant alternatives, namely, to dismiss an executive who had engaged in unethical behavior or to take punitive action against the executive. Consequently, although the board seemed to prefer one of the two options, it delayed formally making and announcing its decision until it was sure it had considerable support for its decision.

Approach-avoidance conflict also represents a source of delaying a decision. For instance, the policy-making board of a secular social agency serving an immigrant population wished to increase its services to the immigrants it was serving. However, several board members were concerned that doing so would divert services from members of one religion in order to provide services to members of another religion, albeit of the same nationality.

Approach-approach conflicts that at face value appear to be most desirable also are a source of decision delay. For instance, a task group charged with hiring a new director of the adult unit of a mental health services center was in the enviable position of having two highly qualified candidates whom they wished to hire. A delay in making the decision occurred. The task group then decided to hire one of the candidates on the basis of affirmative action. However, that candidate at that point had taken another position and was therefore no longer available. The task group then went back later to the other candidate in an attempt to convince the person to take the position.

Another source of decision delay, in addition to conflict, is either actively or passively denying the existence or importance of a decision to be made, thereby contributing to temporarily or permanently avoiding making a decision. Decision delay adds to the possibility of delaying actions by those persons and task groups that are depending on the decision and the foreclosing of the task group's decision making. The task group risks losing power and in extreme situations will find its maintenance or survival at risk within the social service agency. Decision delay also subjects the task group to increased stress from internal and external sources. For example, a task group of social workers denied that it had to comply with accreditation requirements for the agency and delayed reviewing agency programs, with the result that the accreditation of the agency was jeopardized. Consequently, the task group was dismantled, and the status of the members in the agency was jeopardized as well.

Decision Transfer

Harry Truman had a sign that said, "The buck stops here." Jimmy Carter also had the motto in his presidential office. Taking responsibility for making decisions is a sign of character, not only of presidents but of task groups. Ideally, the task group will make the decision itself. Nevertheless, under some circumstances, such as when confronted with a difficult issue, task groups occasionally exercise the option of transferring the making of a decision to another person or organized body. In some respects, decision transfer is superior to ignoring or avoiding the decision at all costs in that decision making may actually occur within the organization, if not by the task group itself. Is decision transfer justifiable? Yes, if that other person or task group is an appropriate and competent decision-making body, in which case the transfer or referral of decision making generally reflects well on the task group. However, a significant hazard is that the task group that transfers decision making will be perceived either as shirking its responsibilities in making difficult decisions or as incompetent. Although the transfer or referral of one or a few decisions during a long period of time can usually be negotiated with little damage to the task group, transfer or referral of decision making on a continuing basis bears with it the hazard of a reduction in decision-making authority and power of the task group. For example, at a mental health agency a task group that considered making a decision relating to the supervision of interns referred the decision to the director of training. To make sure that the task group would be perceived competently, its leader discussed the transfer with a superior at the agency who then approved the action.

Large task groups frequently refer decisions to subgroups as a way of proceeding through their agenda and for decisionmaking action to take place. For example, a large hospital social service department wanted to plan a party for two members who were retiring and referred the decision making and planning for the event to a smaller group of volunteers.

ALTERNATIVE DECISION-MAKING TECHNIQUES

Nominal Group Technique

The nominal group technique (NGT) makes use of a reduced group discussion in an attempt to improve the accuracy of a task group that is working to reduce cognitive conflict (Rohrbaugh, 1981, 1988). In nominal groups persons perform tasks individually and their productivity, as in generating ideas, is combined. In standard (also called *alone*) nominal groups persons do not interact with one another. In *together* nominal groups persons sit together in the same room.

The following is an example of the use of nominal groups with adolescents at risk for sexually transmitted diseases (STDs). First, the leader reminded the adolescents that the purpose of the meeting was to find out about their ideas about STDs and to answer their questions. The adolescents were told that the meeting would last about one hour. Second, the leader put a large piece of paper up on the wall so that all could see it. A discussion question, "Why do you think teenagers think they won't get STDs?" was written on the large paper as well as on the tops of sheets of paper that were passed out to the adolescents. The adolescents were then asked to write down the first four answers that they thought of. They were given 5 minutes for the activity. Third, the leader asked the adolescents to choose and read their own best responses. All the chosen responses were then written on the posted paper for everyone to see. Fourth, the leader asked the adolescents to make sure that their ideas appeared on the poster. Then the ideas were read aloud, and the ideas were clarified, combined, and rewritten, with the group agreeing to the wording of the unique responses. Fifth, the leader asked the adolescents to rank-order the four ideas on the combined list that they thought were the best ones. Sixth, the health educator was introduced, informational pamphlets were distributed, and a discussion was held about STDs.

Brainstorming

Developed by Osborn (1957), brainstorming is a creative technique that allows for the development of many decision alternatives through the creation of a synergistic group effect (Stewart & Shamdasani, 1990). Unlike the nominal group technique, brainstorming is characterized by interpersonal interaction and stimulation and so is familiar to people. Unstructured brainstorming, which is practiced by many task groups, consists of a loose method of attempting to develop ideas in a free manner. In contrast, structured brainstorming (Van Gundy, 1987) is administered using the following guidelines that are presented to the task group members by the leader, often in a statement preceding the actual brainstorming session.

One, the quantity of ideas developed is important. In other words, the more ideas mentioned the better. The underlying assumption is that of many ideas that are mentioned, at least a few will be useful.

Two, judgments of quality are not made; criticism of ideas is withheld. The assumption is that criticism can inhibit the presentation and production of ideas by group members and stifle the creative flow.

Three, ideas can be piggybacked or joined on to one another. This step involves the creative combination of novel ideas with those already presented, thereby making use of the material present in the group process.

Four, wild, unusual, and outrageous ideas are acceptable. Mentioning that there will not be a censorship in regard to ideas gives permission for members to feel free in presenting any and all ideas to the group. The assumption is that the presentation of unusual ideas will have the effect of allowing members who might be constrained to increase their participation and presentation of other ideas.

To many members of task groups, brainstorming is an enjoyable exercise (Rawlinson, 1981) that represents a departure from more constricted processes that tend to constrain participation or at least funnel it in a highly ordered manner. Because of the use of a creative approach and the removal of censorship, brainstorming is claimed to increase the number of ideas available to the group for a decision (Osborn, 1957), of which some are likely to be high quality. However, research studies show that brainstorming groups are significantly less productive in quality and quantity of ideas than are nominal groups (Taylor, Berry, & Block, 1958). Smaller size brainstorming groups without the presence of an authoritative observer that allow members to write down their contributions are likely to compensate for this productivity loss (Mullen, Johnson, & Salas, 1991). Research suggests that note taking with collective assessment increases productivity (Diehl & Stroebe, 1991).

Social Judgment Analysis

Social judgment theory explains how cues (information items) relate to criteria, which reflect the true state about which judgments are made, and how information is used in judgment (Brehmer & Joyce, 1988; Hammond, Stewart, Brehmer, & Steinmann, 1986). The relationship between the cues and the judgments made by an individual or task group in repeated judgment situations is the judgment policy of the individual or group (Gigone & Hastie, 1993).

Social judgment analysis (SJA) is a relatively new type of small group process that is designed to aid in the recognition and resolution of cognitive conflicts. Typically, members of SJA groups are provided with graphic illustrations (e.g., pictures, often computer-generated) of their judgment policies as individuals. The group members then typically compare their individual judgment policies in a free manner until they reach agreement about an overall group judgment policy that resolves any differences among their individual policies.

AFTER THE DECISIONS ARE MADE

Decision Confidence

The confidence that task group members have in one or more aspects of the decisions that have been made by the group, including the decision process, its implementation, and consequences, is likely to be enhanced by the use of voting procedures that are clear and evident to the members. In many task groups the regular use of formal procedures promotes a sense of equity among the members. Furthermore, individuals have greater confidence in decisions arrived at by consensus than by other methods, including majority rule (Gero, 1985). Confidence in the decision process is likely to lead to confidence with the decision product, which in turn is likely to lead to confidence with the decision implementation. For example, a policy-making group developing social services for the elderly had a strong belief in the integrity of its process and therefore was very supportive in making its recommendations about the development of new community service arrangements for the elderly.

Announcing and Publicizing Decisions

Ordinarily, rapidly following the making of a decision, the task group announces and publicizes it, with informal communication sometimes preceding formal communication. However, delays occur to protect the task group members from the anticipated consequences of announcing a controversial or unpopular decision and to allow time to build support for the decision from sources external to the task group. For example, a task group in an alcoholism treatment agency decided to invite to a meeting that it was sponsoring the representatives from an organization with which it had been competitive in seeking funds. Yet the task group waited until it could secure financial support from a variety of other organizations prior to announcing its decision to offer the invitation.

Decision Consequences

Making a decision provides a task group with the basis for action. For instance, a fund-raising group was faced with a difficult decision about whether to proceed with investing in a high-priced consultation that could help the agency find future funding. The agency considered its alternatives and decided to bring in a consultant on a limited basis and to proceed with its own fund-raising activities as a way of minimizing costs paid out to external consultants.

However, concern about the potential consequences of making a decision can result in decisions not being made by a task group. Decision consequences include the provision of positive (praise) and negative (punishment) feedback by others who are observing or affected by the decision. For example, a task group in a school decided to improve its ties to higher education by announcing its interest in having guest speakers come in to deliver in-service training workshops for its staff. Consequently, the school administration praised the efforts of the task group. Simultaneously, however, some of the members of a parents group expressed their concern about the influence of "outsiders" on the educational processes at the school.

The implementation of a decision includes actions by social service agencies that are involved in the decision. Also, decisions vary in the scope of their impact on affected populations. For example, a fund-raising agency decided to change its allocation priorities so that some agencies with more urgent requirements would receive greater priority in receiving funds.

Finally, although decision making has an air of finality to it, the decision-making process is such that decisions are at times revisited and modified. For instance, an interagency task group devoted to building and promoting improved communication and cooperation decided to sponsor monthly social gatherings for members of regional social agencies. After several gatherings had taken place the task group met again to consider information that it had gathered about the effectiveness of the gatherings. The task group subsequently decided to revise its schedule for the gatherings to improve the use of resources and enhance the usefulness of the gatherings.

CONCLUSION

The task group is a central site for decision making in the social services. Decisions and decision making have multiple characteristics, conceptual dimensions, and issues, such as the importance of the decision and the speed of decision making. Customary methods of making decisions in task groups include group discussions, consensus, and voting. Decision making has consequences both for the task group that forms the decision and for those affected by its implementation. Although many factors facilitate effective decision making, other factors (obstacles) such as cognitive conflict interfere with it and must be overcome in order to enhance efficient decision making. Alternative decision-making techniques include the nominal group technique, brainstorming, and social judgment analysis. The Delphi technique, along with others, will be discussed in the next chapter, which examines selected decision-making procedures in large task groups.

Chapter 9

LARGE GROUP
DECISION-MAKING
PROCEDURES

Small group decision-making procedures were considered in Chapter 8, and the present chapter elaborates on how selected group decision-making processes are carried out in larger task groups. For useful application in such groups, it is important to perceive which factors help to facilitate the most efficient and effective means of decision making. Lippitt (1978, pp. 81-83) suggested the following eight factors for success:

1. A clear definition of the problem
2. An understanding of who has responsibility for the decision (The concern here is both freedom to act and the degree of responsibility.)
3. Effective communication for producing ideas
4. A group size appropriate for decision making
5. A means of testing differing alternatives
6. Task groups committed to decisions made
7. Leader commitment to the group decision-making process
8. Need for agreement on the procedures and methods for decision making prior to deliberation on the issue

Given that most of the first seven factors have been discussed previously, let us consider the eighth factor, namely, why it is important to determine the procedures to be used prior to deliberation on the issue. One reason is that sometimes the results of the process can be manipulated or skewed by the methods that are used. Consequently, before lines are clearly drawn between opposing factions, the process for reaching the decision should be agreed on. An example of a situation in which this decision-making process had not been discussed occurred with a group of faculty in a graduate school. This group was composed of about 30 faculty members who had been attempting to change the curriculum of their school. A simple majority vote was taken regarding a new curriculum. The plan passed by only one vote. The minority members were discontent with the outcome and insisted that a simple majority vote was not a way to resolve this issue. The group agreed on another decision-making process in which members rank-ordered choices. This new process resulted in a new decision, one that was only partly satisfactory to the members. A compromise agreement had been reached about the method to be used, and although the results were not what anyone "really" wanted, the program was implemented in the next school year. As noted in a study by Toseland, Rivas, and Chapman (1984), outcomes or judgments about effective groups are dependent on what is meant by effectiveness. Some methods are more likely to produce correct answers, others to produce consensus, and still others to produce member satisfaction.

The decision-making procedures described here may be concerned either with presently reaching a specific conclusion or with gathering further information on which to draw a conclusion at a later time. If the procedure used only expands information or reduces the boundaries of possible choices, then parliamentary procedures are ordinarily used to reach a conclusion. This can be illustrated in the use of Phillips 66, the Crawford slip-writing procedure, ideawriting (or brainwriting), and the Delphi technique. All of these procedures may guide the process toward a conclusion but not to one final specific answer. Usually the vote of the large group or a designated panel must be taken, using parliamentary procedure to arrive at a specific decision.

PARLIAMENTARY PROCEDURE

The most familiar process utilized for making decisions in large task groups in the Western world is parliamentary procedure. Historically, this has been the most effective method for making large group decisions and is very much a part of our democratic government. It has traditionally been used as the basic method for decision making in social service and other organizations. As indicated previously, it also is a very basic all-encompassing method used most often in conjunction with other decision-making processes, such as those described in this chapter.

A major authoritative statement of this process is Robert's (1989) *Rules of Order.* Parliamentary procedure is an especially appropriate process for use in large groups because of the formality and structure inherent in a system of this size. Many people's successful experience with it testifies to its value.

Robert's rules structure, order, and direct the movement of the task group toward its goals. Unfortunately, one of the potentially negative consequences of using the procedures is the possible sacrifice of member satisfaction. Some members participating in a task group using this type of process may feel that they did not have sufficient input to influence the outcomes. They may have heard a motion, observed or participated in a very brief discussion of that motion, and finally voted for or against it. In doing so, members may have found that they were a part of the minority vote, thus not influencing the movement of the group in a significant way. Over time, as members find themselves in the minority, feeling unimportant and insignificant in the group process, they are likely to develop dissatisfaction with participation in the group. (See Chapter 6 for more consideration of the minority position in task groups.)

The use of as many subgroups (such as subcommittees) as is feasible allows for maximum participation of each member in a smaller task group. Many opportunities are thereby created for communicating, providing information, sharing opinions, and influencing the functioning of the subgroup. After the subgroup has completed its simple or complex task, the product or report is submitted to the larger body, sometimes with a recommendation for approval. The larger body, using parliamentary procedures, is prepared to further analyze and act on the proposal in a judicious manner.

An important difference between parliamentary procedures and other large task group processes is that parliamentary procedures usually result in specific decisions, answers, products, or outcomes; other processes most often allow for input, opinion, and facts, rather than almost automatically producing the final decision result. After using a group process for gaining input, the total group may move to the use of parliamentary procedures to determine specific results. Or a small committee may receive the reports and, using parliamentary procedures, consensus, or some other method to produce a specific outcome, move toward attaining the goals of the group. In most instances, in order for the large group to produce the best outcome, a combination of decision-making procedures and parliamentary procedures is used.

PHILLIPS 66

The original version of a large task group process involved dividing a large group or audience into units of six persons and allowing them 6 minutes to formulate a question for the speaker (J. Phillips, 1948). Over time and with use, this process, also known as "buzz groups," has been modified and used frequently in a variety of ways. In the modified version the leader often determines the number of persons most appropriate for each small group, and the amount of time to be spent in the group is determined by the task to be accomplished. Sometimes this type of process, if well organized, can be used even with very large groups of several hundred persons. The content for focus in small groups includes role playing (for training purposes), extending the content of the main speaker and applying it to their own situations, and proposing issues of concern to them to be addressed by a speaker or panel. Small groups may also function as listening teams, in which each team listens for certain content in the speaker's presentation and reports back to the larger group (Bradford & Cory, 1951).

An issue in the use of this process is the optimal level of formality and structure of the discussion in the small task groups. Some large-group leaders believe that the small groups or teams function best using unstructured discussions. Maier (1963) stated that consensus is best reached when the group is unstructured; at the same time the quality of ideas may not be as high as when the group is structured. This method allows for verbal interaction but may inhibit some group members, thereby reducing spontaneity. A major difficulty with the unstructured discussion in the small units is that when the entire group reconvenes, it is very difficult to coordinate any reporting back to the others.

However, experience suggests that especially with task groups larger than 30 participants, it is essential to be directive and structured about the outcomes hoped for and expected from each smaller unit. From this perspective, one of the most important procedures in conducting Phillips 66 is to give clear, purposeful instructions. Indeed, the outcome depends on the leader's explicit and concise directions to the group. Such directions prevent confusion, and extra time is not taken by the group to refine their purpose and task. In a very large group, the resolution of these issues likely results in members' satisfaction and their input to the larger group.

Usually, the first specific direction given by the leader is the method to be used to divide the large task group into smaller units. This can be accomplished by a variety of means. The least structured way is to ask the large group to divide itself into groups of a specific number, such as groups of five. Given considerations of time and clarity, other methods are more appropriate for use with very large groups or audiences. Other methods for dividing the group include counting off (for instance, grouping all number ones together); using a color, number, or distinguishing mark on the name tags; grouping people together on the basis of their particular interest, geographic area, or some other commonality; or other methods that help to facilitate the task to be accomplished.

If the small task groups are to meet in separate rooms, the instructions on how to focus the discussion must be given before the groups adjourn to their own rooms. Members are often trying to connect visually with others in their group and attempting to discover the location of their meeting room. The process can remain organized by having assistants for the leader meet with the small groups in their rooms to repeat and further clarify the goals to be accomplished. After the members are clear about the purpose, the assistants leave, allowing the groups to work on their own. According to Maier (1963), another alternative—having the groups remain together in the same room—has advantages in that the noise and activity of the differing units tend to be contagious, thus motivating all of the groups to work harder.

In addition to instructions about content, the leader should also tell the small groups how long they will have to complete the task and how each group's output, product, or decisions will be shared with the larger group. Time allowed for completing the task may vary with the tasks to be accomplished. Generally, a minimum of 20 to 45 minutes is allowed.

A number of ways can be devised for sharing the reports from the small units. Each group may be instructed to select a reporter who will verbally inform the large group of their decisions, often making use of a flip-chart. This process is advantageous if a few small groups are used. However, if there are many small groups, the material may become very repetitious after a few reports have been made.

Another method of sharing thoughts and ideas is to select a recorder who writes the decisions made and gives the list to a panel who synthesizes the reports of all the task groups and presents the total picture to the large group. This way of reporting works well with small groups who are able to relinquish credit for particular ideas to the larger group. However, this method may be dissatisfying to some of the small groups, because they will not be able to claim credit for specific ideas that they have suggested. Fortunately, there are other ways to share thoughts. One related method is for the recorders of each small group to act as the panel and synthesize all of the groups' ideas before reporting them. This method does require time for the synthesis to be completed before information is shared with the large group.

Other methods for sharing ideas may be especially appropriate for use with audiences or very large assemblies. One such method is for each small group to use a chart to report its ideas and decisions in writing, which are then displayed in an area with all of the others, so that during a break, participants are able to view all the major ideas. Another method used with audiences is to take written reports from the small units and later share them by mail with the other participants.

This type of task group process is especially valuable because it involves a large number of people in a discussion. By participating in small groups each person can be heard. It creates a situation in which differences of opinion can be resolved (Maier, 1963). It allows for maximum participation and use of resources. Not only is there potential for each person to state his or her views, but also there are maximum opportunities to tap the best ideas and information of each person in order to deal most effectively with the task.

The usefulness of this process in local agencies, such as community centers or settlement houses in which decisions affecting the total program are made, is illustrated in the following example. In a community center, the director of the teenage program attempted to determine areas of interest and the priority of each for the next year. Through the current program participants, posters, and other means, the director publicized a meeting to determine what the youngsters wanted and how it could be accomplished. Approximately 100 teenagers came to the meeting. The center staff recognized that friends would arrive and sit together and would want to participate together in small groups unless there was a concrete way of determining the group assignment. The staff also believed that it was important to get differing segments of the adolescent population to think and function together. So, they decided to use numbers on the name tags as a means of dividing the large group into buzz groups. In this way the small groups would more likely be composed of differing factions, and the number on the name tag would encourage teenagers to attend the proper group. Instructions were given to the groups of five, all of which were to remain in the large room together. They were to decide what activities they wanted, to prioritize them, and to discuss how and when the two top priorities could be accomplished. After the 20 groups met for the specified period of time, the leaders of each group met to share ideas and attempt to reach some conclusions. These would be shared with the participants at a later time after a panel had organized and synthesized the ideas.

CRAWFORD SLIP WRITING

The focus of this type of process, which can be used with very large task groups up to or even more than 5,000 people (Van Gundy, 1988), is to bring out as many good ideas as possible and perhaps to gain some sense of group consensus or at least some commonality in ideas. Each person in the group is given a scratch pad or a stack of 25 3×5 cards. A problem statement, which is open-ended so that a variety of responses may be given, is read to the group. For instance, the question may be "How can we . . .?" or "How to . . . ?" Participants are asked to write one idea on each slip without considering the priority or importance of each.

After 5 to 10 minutes, the individuals are asked to stop writing and the statements are collected. A task force is appointed to evaluate and sort the ideas. Usually, the best ideas are sorted into workable proposals.

Several advantages of the Crawford slip-writing process have been identified by Van Gundy (1988). One major advantage is that this method generates a large number of ideas. Van Gundy estimated that 90% of the participants will write five or more ideas. Ten minutes is a very short time in which to produce so many suggestions. Using a task group in this way speeds up the planning process in decision making. An additional advantage is that this method can be used with groups of any size. Seating arrangements are not an obstacle to its use. Total group participation is maximized, and there is a good possibility of discovering new solutions and ideas.

Inevitably, there are also some disadvantages in the use of this process. One dilemma is created by the coordinating effort required to sort and categorize the ideas that have been submitted. The ideas come primarily from individuals and may not be as well developed as they would be if they had emerged in small groups or in some other way. Feedback concerning the outcome of this process can become an obstacle if participants have not been told what to expect. They may become resentful and dissatisfied if there are not timely reports of outcomes precipitated by the use of this process.

The Crawford slip-writing process may be conceptualized as a brainstorming session with a large task group. (See Chapter 8 for a discussion of brainstorming as a small group decision-making procedure.) The following example of a community meeting demonstrates this process. The businesses in a small community were located on a main road until a bypass was constructed. As a result of this change, the economic level of the people living in the community declined. The community has a sum of money that could be spent and a 50-acre piece of land that could be utilized. They wish to draw the travelers from the bypass into the town. In a town meeting, Crawford slip writing could be used to get a wide variety of ideas about how to accomplish this with the existing resources. The question for the participants in this group might be: "With this sum of money and 50 acres of land, what are ways that we could attract travelers from the bypass into our town?" After the slip writing is done, a committee that is representative of the major interests in town sorts and identifies one or more proposals to be presented and acted on at a later time.

IDEAWRITING OR BRAINWRITING

Ideawriting (Moore, 1987) or brainwriting (Van Gundy, 1988) is a method that involves dividing a large task group into smaller groups for idea building, that is, developing and generating ideas and decision making. It is important to do some pre-meeting preparation before using the ideawriting or brainwriting process. First, a decision must be made to determine whether all members will respond to the same stimulus or will choose from a list of options. If one question is to be used for everyone, it should be tested with others before being used with the large group. If a list of stimulus items is used, it must be selected, printed on a sheet of newsprint, and prepared for display.

Preparation involves the acquisition and use of both necessary and optional supplies, because the procedure can be done up to a specific point and stopped or the process may move to another level, depending on the desires of the leaders. Supplies used for the procedure are large pads of paper, pencils, pens, large tables, and chairs. Other items that are often used include flip-charts or easels, newsprint, masking tape, and felt-tip pens.

When the large task group meets, the leader makes an opening statement. The participants are told of the importance of the task and how the results of their efforts will be used. The leader identifies the basic steps of the ideawriting process and tells the participants that the work should be done in silence. The participants are given a time limit to complete the task, which is usually 15 to 30 minutes.

The large task group is then divided into small groups of three to six persons, with an ideal size being three or four participants. One person in each group serves as a group leader. The group leader is appointed by the large group facilitator, selected by the small group, or moved into this role by chance. For example, as a result of counting off to form small groups, the person may be number one, and the large group leader may designate all number ones as small group leaders.

In the first step of the specific procedures for ideawriting or brainwriting, each small group participant writes his or her name in the upper right-hand corner of a large sheet of paper. At the top of the paper each participant writes triggering questions that must be answered before the main issue can be resolved. Following the questions, each participant lists responses to the queries. This process of responding to each item requires 10 to 15 minutes and should be done quickly, silently, and independently.

The next step in ideawriting or brainwriting is to place all of the worksheets from the small task group in the center of the table. Each person selects someone else's worksheet and, after reading it silently, reacts to it by writing additional comments. Then the worksheets are again placed in the center of the table and the process is repeated until everyone has responded to everyone else in the small group.

If the task group uses a set of stimulus items, the basic process is the same. The members of the small group either select or assign the items for each person. (Two or more members may duplicate each other's work.) The next major step is that the worksheets are placed on the table and exchanged by the members. Responses to others' worksheets may include criticizing weaknesses, adding other suggestions, qualifying what that person said, and offering a solution of one's own.

The small task group process may be completed at this time by requesting that the worksheets be left with monitoring teams who will report back at a later time, or the worksheets may be processed immediately. If the material is to be processed immediately, the participants return to their small groups. Each person reads the comments on her or his pad and reports them to the other group members for discussion. After discussion, each member summarizes the issues and ideas. The group then summarizes its efforts on a single sheet of newsprint, which will be used to report back to the large group. A person may be appointed to make the report to the large group using the newsprint for a summary of ideas. The time required for the latter process to take place varies, depending on the content and the number of small group participants.

After the reports have been heard, the large task group holds a discussion to refine the material further and then reaches a decision. The parliamentary process is often used in order to facilitate decision making by the large group.

The use of parallel small groups working on the same task at the same time is efficient and productive. Another important advantage is that it allows one leader to facilitate the work of a large number of people. This process allows all members an equal opportunity to express ideas. Also, groups are more effective if the members have opportunity to think and to clarify ideas by writing them down before contributing to the work of others and discussing. Furthermore, persons are more willing to participate and share ideas if they are not forced into a win-lose, zero-sum position (Moore, 1987). However, time and circumstances do not always permit this to happen.

An advantage of the ideawriting or brainwriting method is that it helps prevent one member from dominating the task group because there are ample opportunities for everyone to express ideas. Contributions tend to be made by everyone, and the status factor that influences others is minimized because the initial focus is more on ideas expressed by the written word than on the personality of the communicator. Indeed, even the chairperson in the small group has relatively little authority in the process.

When the task group is large and the time is short, this method is especially useful because it enables unacquainted individuals to work effectively. Social norms dictate that when individuals enter a group of persons whom they do not know, regardless of the instructions given, the first order of business is an effort to get acquainted. Group participants are concerned about the personality characteristics or psychosocial aspects of the others and about how they are seen by the others and how they fit into the group. The ideawriting or brainwriting method clearly directs the attention of the participants away from themselves and others and toward the task as a primary focus.

Some clearly identified limitations exist in the use of the ideawriting or brainwriting method. First, participants must be willing to express themselves in written form, and some participants may have concerns about writing legibly and spelling correctly. To participate in a meaningful way requires skills in writing clearly and succinctly. The method tends to concretely commit the person expressing the opinion to a point of view early in the decision-making process. Moore (1987) suggested that these procedures are most appropriate to use with professionals and should be used with caution with citizen groups. Another limitation of the method is that it precludes exploration of the relationships between and argumentation of the issues.

An example of how ideawriting or brainwriting would be very useful in decision making is presented in the following situation. Eight YMCAs acquired a piece of land to be used as a camping site by members of all eight agencies, which joined together in the Southwestern Camping Association. The major questions were: Specifically, how will this land be used for camping? What facilities will be required? How will time be scheduled for campers? The land had just been donated, so communication among the staff in regard to its use had yet to take place. Staff who potentially would be involved in camping programs in each agency were called to a meeting to begin to make these decisions. All of the full-time professionals working with the children and teenage program were included.

Forty-three people attended the meeting. The facilitator determined that all the participants should address the same question about use of the property. The ideawriting process was used and the group was divided into groups of four persons with a mix of representatives in each small group.

The planning group for the meeting had carefully explored and considered whether the task group should be stopped after the ideawriting or whether the process should move on to the reporting step. The method was expected to enable the participants to express some unique and original thoughts. Having participants respond to each other in writing introduced some reality-based constraints, added ideas, and provided feedback. The planners believed that stopping the group at this point would frustrate the members because they would want to know what the other small groups were thinking and doing. The land issue was an important one that would affect the job responsibilities of each person. In addition, some of the staff had traveled several miles to attend this session and would be very dissatisfied with leaving the issue unresolved.

Some of the following reasons for wanting to discontinue the process were identified: The planning group wanted more time to think and plan before members committed themselves to an opinion and began to form coalitions or pressure groups. They also wanted the views of board members and of the organizational constituency before moving too far along in decision making.

The planning group decided to have the small task groups continue and then report back to the larger group. The small groups discussed and negotiated their proposals and attempted to reach an agreement. With the help of a reporter and a newsprint outline, each small group presented their ideas. After all the ideas were heard, there was some discussion of the possibilities. Another meeting was scheduled for further refinement of ideas. Copies of the small group proposals and minutes of the discussion that followed were mailed to each participant for further study and consideration before the next session.

DELPHI TECHNIQUE

The Delphi technique has been used to assess current needs, to gain expert opinion while clarifying minority opinion, and even to attempt to predict the future. "It is a creative, futuristic, and sometimes controversial tool that gives each participating individual equal input into the reaching of consensus, although that person may be miles apart from and perhaps unacquainted with the other participants" (Bunning, 1979, p. 174).

The origins of this unique and engaging technique were developed at the Rand Corporation in the early 1950s. The root purpose of the technique was to obtain group opinions about national defense issues, with the name *Delphi* coming from the oracle of the Greek god Apollo. As noted by Pfeiffer (1969), the technique "provides for an impersonal anonymous setting in which opinions can be voiced without bringing 'experts' together in any kind of face-to-face confrontation" (p. 155). The process is intended to create a group consensus through a series of three or four questionnaires. The purpose of this technique is to gain and develop ideas that are based on reason and not skewed by the "bandwagon effect" of majority opinion (Dalkey & Helmer, 1963, p. 465).

The specific procedures used depend on the content to be studied and the expected outcomes. A set of mailed questionnaires is used to contact the respondents. After the first set of opinions or feedback is received, another set of questionnaires is mailed to refine the opinions. This continues for three or four rounds. Generally, the intent of the method is described by deBrigard and Helmer (1970) as:

1. Elicit brief statements regarding developments in their field.
2. Offer these opinions to other members of the group for their feedback.
3. Develop a set of expectations without argument or debate.

The goal of this procedure is to develop consensus on an opinion. If consensus is reached, it is generally believed that this judgment is more valid because of the agreement of several individuals. Gordon and Ament (1969) suggested that even when consensus is not attained, this method may be useful in identifying differing schools of thought as the opinions begin to polarize.

The selection of a panel of experts is crucial in implementing the Delphi technique. Although guidelines for determining the number of experts for the panel vary from a handful to as many as 140, 15 or 20 carefully selected respondents are usually adequate to provide a broad range of opinion (Bunning, 1979). The professional station and reputation (e.g., researcher, professor, lecturer, author, editor) are criteria often used to define experts (Bunning, 1979). An initial commitment to cooperate in this process is elicited from the participants.

Designing the questionnaire is also critical in carrying out the Delphi technique. The number of questions on the initial questionnaire should be very limited, and the space allowed on the form for the response should be relatively small (two to four lines). In later questionnaires the material can be expected to expand, so it is important to be brief initially. The material from the first questionnaire provides the raw data for the next set of questions for the respondents. Using and editing this raw data are the most difficult tasks involved in this technique. A great deal of judgment is used in analyzing the content from the panel respondents, making this task crucial to the success of the technique. Often an editorial panel of persons who are familiar with the subject matter is used in this step. Complications such as semantics, differences in terminology, and even unreadable hand-writing habitually intrude.

After the administration of the first questionnaire, each succeeding one is based on the material obtained from the prior questionnaire. Often each set of questions is more specific and refined than the previous set. Usually the last questionnaire produces the greatest respondent attrition because of factors such as respondent ennui and, occasionally, increasingly compli-cated questions.

Although usually three rounds of questionnaires are used in the Delphi technique, a fourth round is sometimes used in an attempt to gain consen-sus. The final task is to develop a summary of the data for the expert participants and others. This report usually prioritizes the opinions of the members and indicates the number who disagreed with each statement. There is also a summary of the minority opinion. The purpose of this report is to give feedback to the participants in regard to the opinions of other experts—a professional courtesy.

A major area of concern in using the Delphi technique is the return rate of the questionnaires. Unlike studies that require only one set of responses, the Delphi technique requires at least three sets of responses, so the rate of return becomes more crucial with each round. Attempts to improve the rate of return include obtaining a commitment from the respondents to carry through with the total process. After this initial step, it is often useful to determine and announce an expected turnaround time, such as 10 days (Bunning, 1979). At this time, a second copy of the questionnaire is sent with an individualized cover letter and an indication of urgency, such as a red stamp saying *rush* or *urgent* on the envelope. Also, the use of a self-addressed stamped envelope and a coded identification number for anonymity is helpful in promoting continuing participation.

Before making a decision about the use of the Delphi technique, it is important to identify and weigh its advantages and disadvantages. The major advantages of the Delphi technique are that it focuses attention on the issue, does not require geographical proximity, tends to minimize personality characteristics of the experts and group process dynamics, minimizes group pressure on individual opinions, allows each respondent equal opportunity for influence, and provides precise documentation of the data used (Enzer, Little, & Lazer, 1971). The greatest advantage in the use of the technique is that it avoids the pitfalls of public group discussion (Pyke, 1970). Group dynamics such as peer pressure, polarization of opinions, and psychosocial characteristics and personality traits do not influence the opinions of other participants. Researchers have found the results of the Delphi technique to be significantly more accurate than those obtained at an open conference (Campbell, 1966; Uhl, 1971).

The Delphi technique does have its limitations, however. First, it uses subjective judgments based on the opinions of experts rather than more objective data (Weaver, 1971). Second, disagreement reigns about who is an expert. Third, the Delphi technique cannot be as scientific as other areas associated with technological changes (Weaver, 1971). In essence, the experts require material to stimulate thinking (Bernstein, 1969), and there is a heavy expenditure of time in completing the questionnaires (Weaver, 1971).

The Delphi technique has a wide range of application (Bunning, 1979). Its usefulness in social service agencies includes planning at an administrative level. In long-range planning, social service organizations such as hospitals, family service agencies, and youth programs wish to tap the opinions of experts regarding the future of social services. For example, the National Association of Settlements and Centers established a new research division and was interested in publishing reports that would be helpful to the staff in making decisions about social problems that they could expect to confront in the future. The panel divided the list of centers according to the type of population served and whether clients lived in metropolitan or rural areas.

Focusing on the centers serving the metropolitan clients, the panel determined that the executive director of each center was in the best position to be knowledgeable about and to understand that community over time, so the directors served as the experts. After receiving a commitment to cooperate in this process from each expert, a first questionnaire was developed, as follows (adapted from Bunning, 1979):

Delphi Project Future Emphasis
Questionnaire I

The research division of the National Association of Settlements and Centers is soliciting your expert opinion about issues and concerns of your population of clients that can be expected to be of primary concern *in the next three years.* You and other experts across the country have been selected because of your knowledge of your community and its special issues and because of your stated willingness to participate in this Delphi study. Please take a few moments now to complete this brief questionnaire and return it at your earliest convenience.

1. In your community, what do you see as major areas of concern?
2. In your community, what do you see as becoming a major area of concern in the *next three years?*

After the data from this questionnaire have been studied by a panel, a new questionnaire is developed. This second set of questions is used to attempt to develop a consensus of opinion of the experts.

Delphi Project Future Emphasis
Questionnaire II

The following list represents potential present and future issues in your communitiy that you have identified. These listings are the edited results of the responses provided by you and other experts in Questionnaire I. Please rate each item according to the following scale by circling the appropriate priority response.

1—highest priority, definitely the greatest area of concern

2—high priority, certainly a great concern

3—medium priority, a possible area of real concern

4—low priority, a doubtful major area of concern

5—lowest priority, a highly doubtful area of major concern

Present areas of concern are:

1. economic condition of the families	1	2	3	4	5
2. use of drugs	1	2	3	4	5
3. crime and violence	1	2	3	4	5

Future areas of major concern are:

1. further decline of the family	1	2	3	4	5
2. violence of the adolescent girl	1	2	3	4	5
3. child care	1	2	3	4	5

After the data from the second questionnaire are collected and tabulated, a third questionnaire is created to provide feedback on the majority views of the experts, thereby allowing the respondents to either join the majority or state a minority opinion.

CONCLUSION

This chapter has discussed five large group decision-making procedures: parliamentary procedure or Robert's Rules of Order, Phillips 66 or buzz groups, Crawford slip writing, ideawriting or brainwriting, and the Delphi technique. The procedures vary in regard to amounts of interaction, verbalization, and expertise required of the participants, from those that are very social (Phillips 66 or buzz groups) to those marked by an absence of direct contact between the participants (Delphi technique). Two techniques (Crawford slip writing and ideawriting or brainwriting) are intermediate in regard to interaction, verbalization, and expertise required. Parliamentary procedure or Robert's Rules of Order require a high amount of expertise for the most effective participation of members of large task groups.

In large group decision making, practitioners consider the nature of the task group they are working with, including its purpose, goals, and the problem to be dealt with; compare the results they expect to achieve by using the various methods; and determine which technique is the most appropriate for their use. The following chapter discusses ways of evaluating the process and outcome of task groups.

Chapter 10

METHODS OF EVALUATING COMPOSITION, PROCESS, AND OUTCOME IN TASK GROUPS

Task groups have multiple functions, including decision making, problem solving, and evaluation. The purpose of this chapter is to consider the evaluation function and apply it to the composition, process, and outcome of task groups. Task group evaluation refers to an evaluation of the processes or outcomes of the task group carried out either by the task group or by other parties and the use of evaluation methods and procedures by the task group to fulfill its other functions, that is, decision making and problem solving. Task groups have a dual focus in evaluation: inward, that is, evaluating their own performance in carrying out their functions, and outward, that is, evaluating other individuals or task groups.

Virtually all task groups engage in evaluation activities. Task groups that carry out evaluation activities are likely to be perceived inside as well as outside of the task group as more rigorous and effective than those that do not carry out such activities. Task groups that carry out evaluation activities tend to operate according to accepted norms of accountability and utilize established administrative procedures, contemporary models of decision making and problem solving, and novel methods of systematic practice.

Task group evaluations vary in regard to the nature of the phenomena being evaluated; the type of evaluation (e.g., qualitative or quantitative); the scale, size, and complexity of the evaluation; organizational interrelationships; and the distribution, spread, and publication of the evaluation findings. Complex task group evaluations are designed, implemented, and analyzed by a combination of individuals, subgroups, and entire task groups (such as teams) who are in communication. The success of the evaluation depends on the motivation, coordination, and competencies of the participants in the evaluation process.

Task group evaluation is a process in which information is gathered, processed, and used to fulfill other task group functions, and the informational products are dispersed to the task group's external environment. The task group is responsible for collecting the appropriate amount and types of information. For example, a policy-making task group in a child welfare agency was charged with determining how the agency ought to be providing services to deal with increased anecdotal reports of child sexual abuse. The task group gathered information about the incidence and prevalence of the problem at the national, state, and local levels through a series of research activities involving data collection from published and unpublished sources and interviews with experts on the problem. Then the task group analyzed and synthesized the information into a report containing a series of recommendations for the further development of preventive and interventive social services that were ultimately distributed within the agency and then to other relevant persons and agencies.

In addition to being an information process, task group evaluation is a political process that is concerned with addressing politically relevant questions through formulation and discussion and that has political implications because evaluation results affect involved constituencies. For example, a task group in a family service agency organized an evaluation of its services to target population groups in order to determine how well it was serving such groups. When the task group discovered that it served most groups well, it wished to publicize the fact. However, the task group had to deal with the politically sensitive finding that one target population group within its mandate was clearly being underserved. Indeed, that finding allowed the task group to recommend a number of actions to improve the program activities for the underserved group.

PURPOSES OF EVALUATION

Evaluation is akin to assessment in that it involves a measured consideration of the characteristics or functioning of individuals, subgroups, and task groups. However, as will be explained subsequently, the purposes of task group evaluations are broader than the purpose of assessment, which includes gathering information in order to formulate the difficulties of a client system in order to help the clients.

Furthermore, like research, task group evaluations include the collection, analysis, and interpretation of data about individuals, subgroups, and task groups. Task group evaluations are related to clinical and programmatic research methods and bear a relationship to evaluation research methodology in their focus on effectiveness and outcome (Weiss, 1972). In regard to the concern with both process and outcome and the use of design and data collection instruments that should meet criteria of validity, reliability, and utility, task group evaluations are also related to psychotherapy research methodology (Williams & Spitzer, 1984). Ideally, raters should receive training to improve the consistency of their observations, and rater performance should be evaluated (Castorr, Thompson, & Ryan, 1990). Furthermore, when conducted as a research activity, evaluation methods are conceived of as being part of developmental research or evaluation research (Thomas, 1984). In addition, quasi-experimental and to some extent experimental designs tend to be used (Campbell & Cook, 1979; Campbell & Stanley, 1963). Frequently, one-shot case studies are used in practice, with many constraints on their validity. Process evaluations attain greater rigor if they are conducted within the context of single-system research evaluation design (Kazdin, 1982).

However, in contrast to research, the purpose of which is to advance the state of knowledge, task group evaluations are primarily designed and carried out to measure the attainment of social service objectives. Nevertheless, task group evaluations are sometimes carried out in conjunction with developmental research projects whose purpose is to expand practice knowledge. For example, a university-based researcher worked to further the knowledge about which interventions would be likely to improve the marital stability of low-income families. Through the use of task groups, the researcher evaluated the current service capabilities of family service agencies to help low-income families with marital difficulties.

Evaluation encompasses the processes of discovering, uncovering, and determining the process, impact, and effectiveness of task groups. Task group evaluations of extant or formed task groups involve a series of evaluation questions (which may be routine or novel) that culminate in results and conclusions. For example, in a child guidance and evaluation clinic, administrative task groups asked each discipline to make monthly reports of client activities.

The results of task group evaluations tend to vary, with both expected and unexpected results. For example, in a large public welfare agency an evaluation of service provision revealed that some of the workers had considerably higher caseloads than others. This surprised some of the administrators but few of the line staff. A study of the factors associated with the variation was subsequently launched to uncover and resolve the discrepancies.

Evaluation serves a variety of purposes, including determining the efficiency and effectiveness of the task group itself and calculating the provision of resources by the group's external environment in helping the group attain its objectives. For example, a task group in a public housing administration was charged with determining the efficiency of a local unit in making available public housing units to homeless clients.

Another set of task group evaluation purposes includes measuring the satisfaction of social service clients. For instance, an evaluation was conducted of an assertiveness training program for women to determine their satisfaction with the way that the meetings were conducted.

Evaluations of task group functioning are often conducted by and for the task group. Task group evaluations also frequently include an examination of the task group's environment. Evaluation purposes include determining, specifying, and documenting the actions and activities of the task group members as well as those of clients and others who are part of the social service delivery system. For example, an administrative staff group in a state mental hospital asked a clinical services unit to provide an accounting of the attendance and participation of clients in ward meetings.

The overt purpose of evaluation activities is related to and is in accord with the publicly stated and socially sanctioned purposes of the task group. For example, the mission of a child welfare agency included arranging adoptions of severely handicapped youngsters. Correspondingly, one of its evaluations included measuring adoptive parents' knowledge of the services it provided. However, in addition to overt and publicly stated purposes, hidden agendas are also often present (see Chapter 6) and sometimes reflect the presence of political forces such as a desire to uncover hidden problems in the task group, remove a task group leader, reduce the power of a task group, or even change its mandate.

TEMPORAL AND SPATIAL CONTEXT OF EVALUATION

The temporal and spatial context of the task group evaluation activities affects the results of the evaluation as well as their interpretation by those inside and those outside of the task group. Temporal and spatial aspects of the task group evaluation include the extent that the evaluation of the task group is public or private, such as who participates in and who observes the conduct of the evaluation. Evaluation activities that occur in full view of persons, such as the members of the task group, other agency personnel, and clients, communicate that the evaluation is open and tend to lend legitimacy to the process. For instance, in one task group the results of an evaluation of the impact of the group on a community were measured in part by means of a questionnaire. The leader scheduled a working meeting and invited community representatives and other persons to open, read, and tabulate the responses. Those community members who came were privy to the evaluation process and felt included in it.

Indeed, the meetings of the task group provide a convenient and appropriate context for evaluation activities, including data collection and sorting, to occur. Evaluation activities occur inside and outside of the actual task group meetings. Time is an important dimension in organizations (Gherardi & Strati, 1988). Evaluations are usually timed so that data collection and other activities occur prior to, during, immediately or soon after, and as a follow-up to task group meetings. For example, evaluation activities include interviews that are conducted prior to and following the meetings. Evaluations tend to involve data collection at the end of a set time period (such as a 12-month period) and at the conclusion of a particular task group project. External evaluators (e.g., from other task groups) tend to meet on their own to plan and carry out evaluations.

Leader functions of monitoring and evaluating include conducting internal evaluations of the task group. Members also participate in evaluation activities as part of the group process. The implementation of evaluation activities is influenced by the attitudes of leaders and members toward the evaluation process and instruments, which in turn are influenced by emotional responses such as feeling stimulated, challenged, or even threatened (Beggs, Mouw, & Barton, 1989). For example, in one task group some of the members questioned the appropriateness of using any formal instruments. When other members supported such use, a discussion ensued about the task group's collection of data and the group's reliance on professional judgments. In addition to those evaluations carried out within and by the task group, some evaluations are conducted by persons, groups, and organizations external to the task group; in such circumstances outside evaluators tend to review the work of the group.

TYPES OF TASK GROUP EVALUATIONS

Needs Assessment and Composition Evaluations

Three types of evaluation—composition, process, and outcome—tend to occur in task groups. Although process and outcome are mainstays of evaluation, the composition of the task group, which is an important aspect of practice, has an evaluation component as well. Prior to group formation, a composition evaluation is conducted of the requirements of the task group. The interactional and activity components of the task group are specified (Vinter, 1985) as a step in recruiting task group members who possess desired qualifications and who represent politically significant constituencies. Most composition evaluations are conducted prior to the meetings of the task group. However, some composition evaluations are conducted after the group that has already formed begins meeting. For ongoing, long-term task groups that have already met for a substantial period of time and that are entering a new phase in their development, such composition evaluations are useful in redirecting the task group, reexamining their activities, reconsidering their membership, and reorienting the members to the mandate of the task group, as in the wake of an earlier process or outcome evaluation.

A needs assessment carried out by the task group precedes the determination of the desired and requisite composition of the task group and provides the basis for the composition evaluation. For example, in an impoverished neighborhood a broad spectrum of prominent local residents formed a committee to discuss the social problems in the area that they were concerned about and to plan for the development of a community center that would attempt to redress such difficulties. After the committee began meeting, it decided that it would plan for the community center's development by conducting a needs assessment, consisting of a survey of residents in the geographical area to be served by the proposed community center. A needs assessment was carried out involving the following steps: identifying a population that required services, examining relevant professional literature, deriving questions about the needs of the population, establishing a survey research methodology for obtaining the requisite information about the population, carrying out the survey research, analyzing the data, and making recommendations in regard to policy formulation and task group implementation.

In composition evaluation, planners and leaders of task groups carry out three activities, sometimes devising and using instruments. The first activity is to record the desired characteristics of members of the task group, including information about institutional and professional affiliations and sociodemographic characteristics. Once a list of desired characteristics is made, the planners and leaders solicit, obtain, and sort out leads about prospective members. Then they interview the potential members, recording the same types of information that were obtained in regard to the desired characteristics of group members and comparing the actual with the ideal. The information gathered about prospective members is compiled, collated, and synthesized in order to determine the overall feasibility of composing the group.

Process Evaluations

Following a needs assessment and composition evaluation, the task group is formed. Process evaluations involve an analysis of the ongoing meetings of the task group, including how such meetings are conducted and the nature of the interaction. Process evaluations, which examine the means by which the task group seeks to achieve its ends, include an examination of the steps or progress made in achieving such ends or products and therefore are related to outcome evaluations. A crucial step in process evaluations is specifying the variables to be measured. Typical process evaluations assess variables related to the functioning of the group, such as cohesiveness, leadership, task orientation, cooperation, decision making, problem solving, and socioemotional aspects including satisfaction and efficiency. Process evaluations examine variables, such as attendance and participation, that are likely to be associated with task group outcomes. For example, in a series of town meetings conducted in a rural area, an evaluation was conducted of how many residents attended, how many spoke publicly, and how satisfied they rated themselves following the meeting.

Process evaluations, which are conducted while the task group is in progress and prior to its ending, tend to occur at regular time periods, such as during or immediately following each meeting. Formal process evaluations employ instruments, such as structured interviews, questionnaires, and ratings scales, that are designed to amass evaluation data in regard to the functioning of the task group on task and interpersonal dimensions. Interview schedules of varying degrees of structure allow prospective and actual members and leaders to answer questions and give their views relating to the process of the group. Although some instruments are originally developed by the task group, others are created, developed, and used by others (C. Garvin, 1986). Formal process evaluations provide objective evidence of the group's performance and are credible to persons and organizations outside the task group.

In contrast, informal process evaluations, which are frequently conducted by participants of task groups, are akin to gathering and communicating anecdotal evidence or information and providing feedback. Informal process evaluations often consist of acquiring a series of impressions, some of which are communicated both within and outside the task group. For example, in a public health agency a task group meeting was conducted prior to distribution of a final report on social service provision. In an informal process evaluation, the task group leader asked the members how they felt about the contributions that had been made by the external consultant from out of state, and a discussion was held at which opinions were voiced.

Process evaluations of task groups rely on data provided and compiled by persons inside and outside the group. Process evaluations include observations of the task group, in whole or in part, by one or more observers.

Self-reports are usually completed by the members but also may be completed by leaders. In self-reports the members or leaders indicate how they are functioning in the task group and how they feel about it.

Instruments used for measuring group process are useful and applicable with task groups. Such measures include those that are used in measuring virtually any and all groups, those used often in task groups, and even some that are used in psychotherapy groups. SYMLOG, a complex system for the multiple level observation of groups, consists of three dimensions or factors—dominance versus submissiveness, friendliness versus unfriendliness, and acceptance versus nonacceptance of authority—and has been widely used in many settings (Polley, Hare, & Stone, 1988). SYMLOG uses adjective rating, interaction scoring, directional profile, interactional matrix, significant relationships, value statement rating forms, and a field diagram (Bales & Cohen, 1979).

There are instruments that measure the decision process of task groups. (See Chapter 8 for a consideration of decision making.) DeStephen and Hirokawa (1988) developed an instrument that measures members' feelings of agreement, satisfaction, and commitment regarding the group decision, the group decision-making process, group member relationships, individual participation in group decision making, and the individual's contributions during decision making. Reagan and Rohrbaugh (1990) created an instrument that measures the effectiveness of group decision processes. Utilizing four perspectives, each of which contains two effectiveness criteria, the instrument focuses on (a) the rational perspective as a goal-centered process and the efficiency of the decision, (b) the political perspective as an adaptable process and the legitimacy of the decision, (c) the consensual perspective as a participatory process and the supportability of the decision, and (d) the empirical perspective as a data-based process and the accountability of the decision.

Also, many instruments are available that measure various aspects of conflict in task groups in organizations. (See Chapter 6 for methods of working through conflicts.) A classic instrument still used is that of Blake and Mouton (1964), which is based on forcing, withdrawing, smoothing, compromising, and confronting or problem solving as means of managing conflict. Putnam and Wilson (1982) developed the Organizational Communication Conflict Instrument, which measures nonconfrontation, control, and solution orientation. The Rahim Organizational Conflict Inventory-II taps compromising, integrating/collaborating, obliging/accommodating, dominating/competing, and avoiding/withdrawing styles of managing organizational conflict (Rahim, 1983). Riggs (1983) created an instrument that measures the flexibility and activity dimensions of conflict. Recently, Morrill and Thomas (1992) created the Disputing Process Instrument, which assesses conciliatory negotiation, third-party mobilization, overt retaliation, covert retaliation, toleration, avoidance, and discipline.

Outcome Evaluations

Outcome evaluations consider how well the task group has performed its functions, carried out its tasks, met its goals, and delivered its products. Outcome evaluations, which tend to be hard and objective, are concerned with determining the success of the task group in achieving desired results.

After the task group has completed its meetings and process evaluations, its outcome evaluation is also likely to conclude. After an outcome evaluation is conducted, it becomes part of the political process within the organizations and communities who are involved with it, thereby determining its acceptability, use, and impact. For example, a task group in a large public child welfare agency was faced with personnel issues concerning recruitment, retention, and staff turnover. The task group responded by evaluating the success of its efforts through a quantitative analysis of personnel change. Although the task group attempted to be systematic and impartial, it was nevertheless critiqued for its choices of data sources, which some observers said were self-interested and biased—a charge refuted by the group.

In addition to formal outcome evaluations, outcome evaluations are frequently made on an informal basis by observers who consider how successful the group has been in meeting its goals. Such informal outcome evaluations tend to supplement formal evaluations rather than replace them. Indeed, some formal outcome evaluations include such qualitative perceptions in their overall evaluation of the task group. For example, the members of a task group that had completed its work on reviewing benefits for employees at a large municipal public welfare agency discussed the findings among themselves at the final meeting of the group for the year.

Typically, outcome evaluations consist of an examination of the task group's functioning at the end of one or more of the following three points. One, the final data collection phase of many task group outcome evaluations occurs at the end of a specified and often considerable period of time (e.g., a school year or a calendar year), after the group has had a chance to make significant progress on its tasks.

Two, an outcome evaluation may occur after the completion of a specified major project, thereby allowing an evaluation of the work that went into the project and its results. Often the impact of the task group is of interest; however, this can usually be best measured after the outcome evaluation has occurred. Such a follow-up evaluation allows for measurement of the effect of the task group decisions, reports, and other outcomes on the task group, related organizations, and constituencies.

Three, an outcome evaluation may occur at the point when the entire task group disbands, which allows for measuring the overall accomplishment of the group (Rose, 1989). However, in situations in which a task group continues to meet over extended time periods (such as years), and given the urgency for attaining evaluation findings, one of the other types of outcome evaluation mentioned previously is likely to be considered in addition to a process evaluation.

Some relatively simple outcome evaluations of task groups involve the collection of data only once, either at the end of the group or at one of the other outcome points. Although such evaluations provide some information about the outcome of the particular task group being evaluated, they are limited in the comparisons that can be made. However, outcome evaluations tend to be more valid if they involve a collection of data at two or more points, such as the beginning and end, thereby allowing for an estimate of the change processes that have occurred within the particular task group (Campbell & Stanley, 1963).

If other outcome information such as normative data or outcome data from other task groups is available, then a comparison can be made to determine the meaning of the outcome data that have been collected. The usefulness of comparing the task group's functioning with that of other task groups is seen in the following example. An interagency task force on child abuse made a comparison of the outcomes of task group functioning among all child abuse prevention teams in the state. The comparison showed that outcomes varied according to region, and the task force launched a study to determine the variables associated with differential outcomes. Outcome evaluations, then, measure variables such as effectiveness and results in regard to decisions made and problems solved.

Working toward group goals tends to increase the task performance of members (Weingart & Weldon, 1991). For addressing the outcome of the group, goal attainment scaling is a useful instrument (Kiresuk & Sherman, 1968). Inevitably, some criticism has been voiced about the statistical properties of goal attainment scaling (Seaberg & Gillespie, 1977); however, the instrument continues to be widely used.

Interview schedules allow for specific information to be obtained in a highly specified content domain and are particularly useful in outcome evaluations. Respondents of survey instruments, interview schedules, and questionnaires tend to be task group members and leaders as well as other parties who contribute to and perceive the outcomes of the task group.

EVALUATION PROCESS

Evaluation is conceptualized as a five-stage process. The first stage involves the identification of the issues to be addressed and questions to be answered through the evaluation. As a formal process, then, task group evaluation at this beginning stage consists of the formulation of one or more evaluation questions. For example, a task group concerned with the development of state mental health policy posed a question about the extent to which information was available about the utilization of mental health services by chronically and severely mentally disordered persons.

Second, during the design stage, methodology for obtaining answers to the evaluation questions is developed. For example, the mental health policy task group decided to use a quasi-experimental design to conduct an internal and external evaluation that would gather the information as well as monitor its own effectiveness as a task group.

Third, the implementation stage involves the administration of instruments to measure and record the data relevant to the evaluation. Frequently, a combination of qualitative and quantitative data is collected. For example, the task group decided to gather the relevant information from public and private mental health facilities and simultaneously to monitor its own success at obtaining such information. It collected information that it then transferred onto evaluation forms it had developed and used goal attainment scaling to monitor its success at obtaining the desired information.

In the analysis stage, the collected data are examined and interpreted to respond to the issues and questions raised earlier in the evaluation process. For example, the mental health task group tabulated the results, had them statistically analyzed with the assistance of a computer, and reviewed their results. The results suggested that the task group was able to gather information from most sectors of the state and that most of the vulnerable populations of chronically and severally mentally disabled persons that they were interested in serving were receiving at least a minimum level of social services, as monitored by a case manager.

The evaluation results form the basis for the conclusions of the evaluation. The last stage consists of preparing a formal evaluation report that describes all parts of the completed evaluation. Policy recommendations are formulated. The conclusions of the evaluation are disseminated and brought to the attention of multiple audiences, including the task group, the agencies involved, and community members and groups. For example, the mental health task group arranged a series of regional meetings in which they presented their findings to mental health consumers, advocates, patient groups, family members and organizations, service deliverers, planners, administrators, policy makers, and legislators.

CONCLUSION

Evaluation has multiple purposes and is relevant for improving the composition, process, and outcome of task groups. This chapter has focused on evaluation as a function and an activity of the task group that helps it carry out its other functions. By culminating in an identification of areas of strength and areas in which the task group should be performing better, evaluation contributes to the effective performance of the group and improves its well-being.

Evaluation is inevitably tied to the external environment. Indeed, the demands for accountability, which often originate in the environment that sustains the task group, are usually fulfilled by evaluation. Concurrent with such external links, the focus of many task group evaluations is inward.

This chapter has considered formal and informal task group evaluations. Task groups may use extant and original instruments in conducting formal evaluations.

Evaluation is understood within the time dimension of the task group and tends to occur at multiple intervals. Evaluation occurs before, during, and after the task group convenes for carrying out its projects. Task group evaluations consist of five stages: issue identification, design, implementation, analysis, and formulation and distribution of results and recommendations.

REFERENCES

Alissi, A. S. (1980). Social group work: Commitments and perspectives. In A. S. Alissi (Ed.), *Perspectives on social group work practice* (pp. 5-35). New York: Free Press.

Alissi, A. S., & Casper, M. (Eds.). (1985). *Time as a factor in groupwork: Time limited group experiences*. New York: Haworth.

Abramson, J. S. (1989). Making teams work. *Social Work With Groups, 12,* 45-63.

Abramson, J. S. (1993). Orienting social work employees in interdisciplinary settings: Shaping professional and organizational perspectives. *Social Work, 38,* 152-157.

Anderson, L. E., & Balzer, W. K. (1991). The effects of timing of leaders' opinions on problem-solving groups: A field experiment. *Group & Organization Studies, 16,* 86-101.

Back, K. (1951). Influence through communication. *Journal of Abnormal Psychology, 46,* 9-23.

Bales, R. F. (1952). Some uniformities of behavior in small social systems. In G. L. Hartley (Ed.), *Readings in social psychology* (pp. 146-159). New York: Holt.

Bales, R. F. (1955). Adaptive and integrative changes as a source of strain in social systems. In A. P. Hare, E. F. Borgatta, & R. F. Bales (Eds.), *Small groups: Studies in social interaction* (pp. 127-131). New York: Knopf.

Bales, R. F., & Cohen, S. P. (1979). *SYMLOG: A system for the multiple level observation of groups*. New York: Free Press.

Bales, R. F., & Slater, P. E. (1955). Role differentiation in small decision-making groups. In T. Parsons & R. F. Bales (Eds.), *Family, socialization, and interaction process* (pp. 259-306). Glencoe, IL: Free Press.

Bales, R. F., & Strodtbeck, F. L. (1951). Phases in problem solving. *Journal of Abnormal and Social Psychology, 46,* 485-495.

Barton, W. A., Jr. (1926). The effect of group activity and individual effort in developing ability to solve problems in first-year algebra. *Educational Administration and Supervision, 12,* 512-518.

Beggs, D. L., Mouw, J. T., & Barton, J. A. (1989). Evaluating gifted programs: Documenting individual and programmatic outcomes. *Roeper Review, 12,* 73-76.

Benne, K. D., & Sheats, P. (1948). Functional roles of group members. *Journal of Social Issues, 4,* 41-49.

Bennett, F. C. (1982). The pediatrician and the interdisciplinary process. *Exceptional Children, 48,* 306-314.

Bernstein, G. B. (1969). *A fifteen year forecast of information processing technology.* Detroit, MI: Management Information Services.

Blake, R. R., & Mouton, J. S. (1964). *The managerial grid.* Houston: Gulf.

Blum, D., & Blum, R. (1991). Patient-team communication. *Journal of Psychosocial Oncology, 9,* 81-88.

Boyd, H. W., Westfall, R., & Stasch, S. F. (1981). *Marketing research: Text and cases.* Homewood, IL: Richard D. Irwin.

Boyd, N. L. (1971). *Play and game theory in group work* (P. Simon, Ed.). Chicago: University of Illinois, Jane Addams Graduate School of Social Work.

Bradford, L., & Cory, S. (1951). Improving large group meetings. *Adult Education, 1,* 122-137.

Brehmer, B. (1976). Social judgment theory and analysis of interpersonal conflict. *Psychological Bulletin, 83,* 985-1003.

Brehmer, B., & Joyce, C. R. B. (Eds.). (1988). *Human judgment: The SJT view.* Amsterdam: North-Holland.

Brickner, M., Harkins, S., & Ostrom, T. (1986). Personal involvement: Thought provoking implications for social loafing. *Journal of Personality and Social Psychology, 51,* 763-769.

Brilhart, J. (1974). *Effective group discussion* (2nd ed.). Dubuque, IA: William C. Brown.

Broome, B. J., & Chen, M. (1992). Guidelines for computer-assisted group problem solving: Meeting the challenges of complex issues. *Small Group Research, 23,* 216-236.

Brown, L. N. (1991). *Groups for growth and change.* New York: Longman.

Bunning, R. L. (1979). The Delphi technique: A projection tool for serious inquiry. In J. E. Jones & W. Pfeiffer (Eds.), *The 1979 annual handbook for group facilitators* (pp. 174-181). La Jolla, CA: University Associates.

Cadoret, A. (1989). Retard de parole et de language: Differents cas de figure et reflexion sur la recherche des causes [Delays in speech and language: Different case types and thoughts on causal research]. *Pratique-des-Mots, 68,* 12-17.

Calder, B. J. (1977). Focus groups and the nature of qualitative marketing research. *Journal of Marketing Research, 14,* 353-364.

Campbell, D., & Cook, T. (1979). *Quasi-experimentation: Design and analysis for field settings.* Skokie, IL: Rand McNally.

Campbell, D. T., & Stanley, J. C. (1963). *Experimental and quasi-experimental designs for research.* Skokie, IL: Rand McNally.

Campbell, R. M. (1966). *A methodological study of the utilization of experts in business forecasting.* Unpublished doctoral dissertation, University of California, Los Angeles.

Cartwright, D., & Zander, A. (1960). *Group dynamics: Research and theory* (2nd ed.). New York: Harper & Row.

Castorr, A. H., Thompson, K. O., & Ryan, J. W. (1990). The process of rater training for observational instruments: Implications for interrater reliability. *Research in Nursing and Health, 13,* 311-318.

Chafetz, P., West, H., & Ebbs, E. (1987). Overcoming obstacles to cooperation in interdisciplinary long term care teams. *Journal of Gerontological Social Work, 11,* 131-140.

Churchman, C. W. (1971). *The design of inquiring systems: Basic concepts of systems and organizations.* New York: Free Press.

Cohen, A. R. (1958). Upward communication in experimentally created hierarchies. *Human Relations, 11,* 41-53.

Collins, B. E., & Guetzkow, H. (1964). *A social psychology of group processes for decision-making.* New York: John Wiley.

Compton, B., & Galaway, B. (1984). *Social work processes* (3rd ed.). Homewood, IL: Dorsey.

Cooley, C. (1918). *Social process.* New York: Scribner.

Coser, L. A. (1956). *The function of social conflict.* New York: Free Press.

Cosier, R. A., & Schwenk, C. R. (1990). Agreement and thinking alike: Ingredients for poor decisions. *Academy of Management Executive, 4,* 69-74.

Courtnage, L., & Smith-Davis, J. (1987). Interdisciplinary team training: A national survey of special education teacher training programs. *Exceptional Children, 53,* 451-458.

Cox, T. H., Lobel, S. A., & McLeod, P. L. (1991). Effects of ethnic group cultural differences on cooperative and competitive behavior on a task group. *Academy of Management Journal, 34,* 827-847.

Coyle, G. L. (1930). *Social process in organized groups.* New York: Richard R. Smith.

Coyle, G. L. (1947). *Group experience and democratic values.* New York: Women's Press.

Coyle, G. L. (1948). *Group work with American youth.* New York: Harper & Brothers.

Coyle, G. L. (1959). Group work in psychiatric settings: Its roots and branches. *Social Work, 4,* 74-81.

Crouch, A., & Yetton, P. (1987). Manager behavior, leadership style, and subordinate performance: An empirical extension of the Vroom-Yetton conflict rule. *Organizational Behavior and Human Decision Processes, 39,* 384-396.

Dalkey, N. C., & Helmer, O. (1963). An experimental application of the Delphi method to the use of experts. *Management Science, 9,* 458-467.

D'Augelli, A. R. (1973). Group composition using interpersonal skills on peer ratings and group cohesion. *Journal of Counseling Psychology, 46,* 531-534.

Davis, L. E. (1986). Group work practice with ethnic minorities of color. In M. Sundel, P. Glasser, R. Sarri, & R. Vinter (Eds.), *Individual change through small groups* (2nd ed., pp. 324-344). New York: Free Press.

deBrigard, P., & Helmer, O. (1970). *Some potential societal developments: 1970-2000.* Middletown, CT: Institute for the Future.

DeStephen, R. S., & Hirokawa, R. Y. (1988). Small group consensus: Stability of group support of the decision, task process and group relationships. *Small Group Behavior, 19,* 227-239.

Deutsch, M. (1969). Conflicts: Productive and destructive. *Journal of Social Issues, 25,* 7-41.

Dewey, J. (1910). *How we think.* Boston: D. C. Heath.

Dewey, J. (1933). *How we think* (rev. ed.). New York: D. C. Heath.

Dewey, J. (1966). *Democracy and education.* New York: Free Press.

Diehl, M., & Stroebe, W. (1991). Productivity loss in idea-generating groups: Tracking down the blocking effect. *Journal of Personality and Social Psychology, 61,* 392-403.

Dore, M. M. (1993). The practice-teaching parallel in educating the micropractitioner. *Journal of Social Work Education, 29,* 181-190.

Ducanis, A. J., & Golin, A. K. (1979). *The interdisciplinary health care team: A handbook.* Germantown, MD: Aspen System Corporation.

Enzer, S., Little, D., & Lazer, F. (1971). *Some societal changes by 1985 and their impact on time/money budget.* Middletown, CT: Institute for the Future.

Ephross, P. H., & Vassil, T. (1987). Toward a model of working groups. *Social Work With Groups, 10,* 11-23.

Ephross, P. H., & Vassil, T. (1988). *Groups that work: Structure and process.* New York: Columbia University Press.

Ephross, P. H., & Vassil, T. (1993). The rediscovery of real-world groups. *Social Work With Groups, 16,* 15-25.

Exline, R. V. (1959). Group climate as a factor in the relevance and accuracy of social perception. *Journal of Abnormal and Social Psychology, 1,* 201-209.

Fandt, P. M., Cady, S. H., & Sparks, M. R. (1993). The impact or reward interdependency on the synergogy model of cooperative performance: Designing an effective team environment. *Small Group Research, 24,* 101-115.

Fatout, M. F. (1992). *Models for change in social group work.* New York: Aldine de Gruyter.

Fern, E. F. (1982). The use of focus groups for idea generation: The effects of group size, acquaintanceship and moderator on response quanitity and quality. *Journal of Marketing Research, 19,* 1-13.

Festinger, L. (1978). Informal communication in small groups. In L. P. Bradford (Ed.), *Group development* (2nd. ed., pp. 137-151). La Jolla, CA: University Associates.

Festinger, L., Schachter, S., & Back, K. W. (1950). *Social pressure in informal groups.* New York: Harper.

Fiorelli, J. S. (1988). Power in work groups: Team members' perspectives. *Human Relations, 41,* 1-12.

Fisher, B. A. (1974). *Small group decision making: Communication and group process.* New York: McGraw-Hill.

Follett, M. P. (1926). *The new state.* New York: Longman, Green.

Garner, H. G. (1988). *Helping others through teamwork.* Washington, DC: Child Welfare League of America.

Garvin, C. (1986). Developmental research for task-centered group work with chronic mental patients. *Social Work With Groups, 9,* 31-42.

Garvin, C. (1987). *Contemporary group work* (2nd ed.). Englewood Cliffs, NJ: Prentice Hall.

Garvin, C. D., & Cox, F. M. (1987). A history of community organizing since the Civil War with special reference to oppressed communities. In F. M. Cox, J. L. Erlich, J. Rothman, & J. E. Tropman (Eds.), *Strategies of community organization* (4th ed., pp. 26-63). Itasca, IL: F. E. Peacock.

Garvin, D. A. (1993). Building a learning organization. *Harvard Business Review, 71,* 78-91.

Gero, A. (1985). Conflict avoidance in consensual decision processes. *Small Group Behavior, 16,* 487-499.

Gherardi, S., & Strati, A. (1988). The temporal dimension in organizational studies. *Organizational Studies, 9,* 149-164.

Gigone, D., & Hastie, R. (1993). The common knowledge effect: Information sharing and group judgment. *Journal of Personality and Social Psychology, 65,* 959-974.

Golembiewski, R. (1962). *The small group.* Chicago: University of Chicago Press.

Goodacre, D. M., III. (1951). The use of sociometric tests as a predictor of combat unit effectiveness. *Sociometry, 14,* 148-152.

Gordon, T. J., & Ament, R. H. (1969). *Forecasts of some technological and scientific developments and their social consequences.* Middletown, CT: Institute for the Future.

Gray, J., & Fryer, G. E. (1991). Physician assistants as members of social service child protection units. *Child Abuse & Neglect, 15,* 415-421.

Greenfeld, D., Diamond, M. P., Breslin, R. L., & DeCherney, A. (1986). Infertility and the new reproductive technology: A role for social work. *Social Work in Health Care, 12,* 71-81.

Gross, E. (1956). Symbiosis and consensus as integrative factors in small groups. *American Sociological Review, 21,* 174-179.

Haines, B., & McKeachie, W. (1982). Cooperative versus competitive discussion methods in teaching introductory psychology. *Journal of Educational Psychology, 58,* 386-390.

Hall, R. H. (1986). Interorganizational or interprofessional relationships: A case of mistaken identity? In W. R. Scott & B. L. Black (Eds.), *The organization of mental health services: Societal and community system* (pp. 147-158). Beverly Hills, CA: Sage.

Hamlin, E. R. (1991). Community based spouse abuse protection and family preservation team. *Social Work, 36,* 402-406.

Hammond, K. R., Stewart, T. R., Brehmer, B., & Steinmann, D. O. (1975). Social judgment theory. In M. F. Kaplan & S. Schwartz (Eds.), *Human judgment and decision processes* (pp. 271-312). New York: Academic Press.

Hammond, K. R., Stewart, T. R., Brehmer, B., & Steinmann, D. (1986). Social judgment theory. In H. K. Arkes & K. R. Hammond (Eds.), *Judgment and decision-making: An interdisciplinary reader* (pp. 56-76). New York: Cambridge University Press.

Hare, A. P. (1952). A study of interaction and consensus in different sized groups. *American Sociological Review, 17,* 261-267.

Hare, A. P. (1976). *Handbook of small group research* (2nd ed.). New York: Free Press.

Hare, A. P., Borgatta, E. F., & Bales, R. F. (Eds.). (1955). *Small groups: Studies in social interaction* (rev. ed.). New York: Knopf.

Harkins, S. G., & Szymanski, K. (1987). Social loafing and social facilitation: New wine in old bottles. In C. Hendrick (Ed.), *Review of personality and social psychology* (pp. 167-188). Newbury Park, CA: Sage.

Hartford, M. E. (1972). *Groups in social work.* New York: Columbia University Press.

Hasenfeld, Y., & English, R. A. (Eds.). (1974). *Human service organizations: A book of readings.* Ann Arbor: University of Michigan Press.

Heap, K. (1977). *Group theory for social workers: An introduction.* New York: Pergamon.

Hemphill, J. K., & Sechrest, L. A. (1952). A comparison of three criteria of air crew effectiveness in combat over Korea. *American Psychologist, 7,* 391.

Henry, S. (1992). *Group skills in social work: A four-dimensional approach* (2nd ed.). Pacific Grove, CA: Brooks/Cole.

Hensley, T. R., & Griffin, G. W. (1986). Victims of groupthink: The Kent State University board of trustees and the 1977 gymnasium controversy. *Journal of Conflict Resolution, 30,* 497-531.

Hirokawa, R. Y., & Scheerhorn, D. R. (1986). Communication in faulty group decision-making. In R. Y. Hirokawa & M. S. Poole (Eds.), *Communication and group decision-making* (pp. 81-92). Beverly Hills, CA: Sage.

Hoffman, L. R. (1979). *The group problem solving process: Studies of a valence model.* New York: Praeger.

Homans, G. C. (1950). *The human group.* New York: Harcourt Brace Jovanovich.

Home, A. M. (1991). Mobilizing women's strengths for social change: The group connection. *Social Work With Groups, 14,* 153-173.

Huber, G. (1980). *Managerial decision making.* Glenview, IL: Scott, Foresman.

Jackson, J., & Harkins, S. (1985). Equity in effort: An explanation of the social loafing effect. *Journal of Personality and Social Psychology, 49,* 1199-1206.

Janis, I. L. (1982). *Groupthink: Psychological studies of policy decisions and fiascoes.* Boston: Houghton Mifflin.

Kane, R. A. (1990). The interprofessional team as a small group. In K. W. Davidson & S. S. Clarke (Eds.), *Social work in health care* (pp. 277-307). New York: Haworth.

Karau, S. J., & Williams, K. D. (1993). Social loafing: A meta-analytic review and theoretical integration. *Journal of Personality and Social Psychology, 65,* 681-706.

Kay, G., Moffatt, C., MacTavish, M., & Lau, G. (1990). The merits of geriatric assessment units: A holistic approach versus the medical model. *Clinical Gerontologist, 10,* 54-57.

Kazdin, A. E. (1982). *Single-case research designs: Methods for clinical and applied settings.* New York: Oxford University Press.

Kelley, H. H. (1951). Communication in experimentally created hierarchies. *Human Relations, 4,* 39-56.

Kerr, N. L. (1985). Motivational choices in task groups: A paradigm for social dilemma research. In H. A. M. Wilke, D. M. Messick, & C. G. Rutte (Eds.), *Experimental social dilemmas* (pp. 1-27). Frankfurt: Verlag Peter Lang.

Keyton, J. (1993). Group termination: Completing the study of group development. *Small Group Research, 24,* 84-100.

Kiresuk, T., & Sherman, R. (1968). Goal attainment scaling: A general method for evaluating comprehensive community mental health programs. *Community Mental Health Journal, 4,* 443-453.

Klein, A. F. (1970). *Social work through group process.* Albany: State University of New York.

Klugman, S. F. (1944). Cooperative versus individual efficiency in problem-solving. *Journal of Educational Psychology, 35,* 91-100.

Konopka, G. (1963). *Social group work: A helping process.* Englewood Cliffs, NJ: Prentice Hall.

Landers, D. M., & Crum, T. F. (1971). The effect of team success and formal structure on inter-personal relations and cohesiveness of baseball teams. *International Journal of Sports Psychology, 2,* 88-96.

Latane, B., Williams, K. D., & Harkins, S. G. (1979). Many hands make light the work: The causes and consequences of social loafing. *Journal of Personality and Social Psychology, 37,* 822-832.

Lazarsfeld, P. F., Berelson, B., & Gaudet, H. (1944). *The people's choice.* New York: Duel Sloan & Pearce.

Lee, S. (1980). Interdisciplinary teaming in primary care: A process of evolution and resolution. *Social Work in Health Care, 5,* 237-244.

Leigh, H. (1987). Multidisciplinary teams in consultation-liaison psychiatry: The Yale model. *Psychotherapy and Psychosomatics, 48,* 83-89.

Lewin, K. (1935). *A dynamic theory of personality.* New York: McGraw-Hill.

Lewis, E. (1989, October). Social change and citizen action: A philosophical exploration for modern social group work [Mimeo]. Paper presented at the 11th Annual Symposium, AASWG, Montreal.

Lewis, E. (1991). Social change and citizen action: A philosophical exploration for modern social group work. *Social Group Work, 14,* 23-34.

Lindeman, E. C. (1921). *The community: An introduction to the study of community leadership and organization.* New York: Association Press.

Lippitt, G. (1978). Improving decision-making with groups. In L. P. Bradford (Ed.), *Group development* (2nd ed., pp. 79-83). La Jolla, CA: University Associates.

Lorge, I. (1955). Problem-solving by teams and by individuals to a field problem at different levels of reality. *Journal of Educational Psychology, 46,* 17-24.

MacIver, R. (1924). *Community.* New York: Macmillan.

Maier, N. (1963). *Problem solving discussions and conferences: Leadership methods and skills.* New York: McGraw-Hill.

Maier, N., & Sashkin, M. (1971). Specific leadership behaviors that promote problem solving. *Personnel Psychology, 24,* 35-44.

Marquis, D. G., Guetzkow, H., & Heyns, R. W. (1951). A social psychological study of the decision-making conference. In H. Guetzkow (Ed.), *Groups, leadership and men* (pp. 55-67). Pittsburgh: Carnegie Press.

Martens, R., & Peterson, J. A. (1971). Group cohesion as a determinant of success and member satisfaction in team performance. *International Review of Sports Psychology, 6,* 49-61.

Mayadas, N. S., & Glasser, P. H. (1986). The changing nature of social group work practice. In P. H. Glasser & N. S. Mayadas (Eds.), *Group workers at work: Theory and practice in the eighties* (pp. 3-10). Totowa, NJ: Rowman & Littlefield.

McKay, M., & Paleg, K. (Eds.). (1992). *Focal group psychotherapy.* Oakland, CA: New Harbinger.

Mehrabian, A., & Diamond, S. G. (1971). Effects of furniture arrangement, props, and personality in social interaction. *Journal of Personality and Social Psychology, 20,* 281-289.

Merton, R. F. (1957). *Social theory and social structure.* Glencoe, IL: Free Press.

Messick, D. M., & Brewer, M. B. (1983). Solving social dilemmas: A review. In L. Wheeler & P. Shaver (Eds.), *Review of personality and social psychology* (pp. 11-44). Beverly Hills, CA: Sage.

Minz, N. (1956). Effects of esthetic surroundings II: Prolonged and repeated experience in a "beautiful" and an "ugly" room. *Journal of Psychology, 41,* 459-466.

Mondros, J. B., & Berman-Rossi, T. (1991). The relevance of stages of group development theory to community organization practice. *Social Work With Groups, 14,* 203-221.

Moore, C. M. (1987). *Group techniques for idea building.* Newbury Park, CA: Sage.

Morgan, D. L., & Spanish, M. T. (1984). Focus groups: A new tool for qualitative research. *Qualitative Sociology, 7,* 253-269.

Morrill, C., & Thomas, C. K. (1992). Organizational conflict management as disputing process: The problem of social escalation. *Human Communication Research, 18,* 400-428.

Morrison, T. (1987). Creating change in abusing families. *Adoption and Fostering, 11,* 25-29.

Moscovici, S., & Mugny, G. (1983). Minority influence. In P. B. Paulus (Ed.), *Basic group processes* (pp. 41-64). New York: Springer Verlag.

Mullen, B., & Baumeister, R. F. (1987). Group effects on self-attention and performance: Social loafing, social facilitation, and social impairment. In C. Hendrick (Ed.), *Review of personality and social psychology* (pp. 189-206). Newbury Park, CA: Sage.

Mullen, B., Johnson, C., & Salas, E. (1991). Productivity loss in brainstorming groups: A meta-analytic integration. *Basic and Applied Psychology, 12,* 3-23.

Mullender, A., & Ward, D. (1991). Empowerment through social action group work: The self-directed approach. *Social Work With Groups, 14,* 125-139.

Munzer, J., & Greenwald, H. (1957). Interactional process analysis of a therapy group. *International Journal of Group Psychotherapy, 7,* 175-190.

Murphy, M. (1959). *The social group work method in social work education.* New York: Council on Social Work Education.

Napier, R. W., & Gershenfeld, M. K. (1983). *Making groups work: A guide for group leader.* Boston: Houghton Mifflin.

Nash, J., Rounds, K., & Bowen, G. L. (1992). Level of parental involvement on early childhood intervention teams. *Families in Society, 73,* 93-99.

Newstetter, W. I. (1935). What is social group work? In *Proceedings of the National Conference of Social Work at the 62nd Annual Session held in Montreal, Canada* (pp. 291-299). Chicago: University of Chicago Press.

Northen, H. (1969). *Social work with groups.* New York: Columbia University Press.

Northen, H. (1988). *Social work with groups* (2nd ed.). New York: Columbia University Press.

Osborn, A. F. (1957). *Applied imagination* (rev. ed.). New York: Scribner.

Patton, B. R., & Giffin, K. (1973). *Problem-solving group interaction.* New York: Harper & Row.

Payne, M. (1982). *Working in teams.* London: Macmillan.

Pepitone, A., & Reichling, G. (1955). Group cohesiveness and expression of hostility. *Human Relations, 8,* 327-337.

Pernell, R. B. (1986). Old themes for a new world. In P. H. Glasser & N. S. Mayadas (Eds.), *Group workers at work: Theories and practice in the eighties* (pp. 11-21). Totowa, NJ: Rowman & Littlefield.

Pfeiffer, J. (1969). *New look at education.* Princeton, NJ: Western.

Phillips, H. U. (1951). *Essentials of social group work skill.* New York: Association Press.

Phillips, J. (1948). Report on discussion 66. *Adult Education Journal, 7,* 181-182.

Pitts, M., Jackson, H., & Wilson, P. (1990). Attitudes, knowledge, experience and behavior related to HIV and AIDS among Zimbabwean social workers. *AIDS Care, 2,* 53-61.

Polley, R. B., Hare, A. P., & Stone, P. J. (Eds.). (1988). *The SYMLOG practitioner: Application of small group research.* New York: Praeger.

Priem, R. L., & Price, K. H. (1991). Process and outcome expectations for the dialectical inquiry, devil's advocacy, and consensus techniques of strategic decision making. *Group & Organization Studies, 16,* 206-225.

Putnam, L. L. (1986). Conflict in group decision-making. In R. Y. Hirokawa & M. S. Poole, (Eds.), *Communication and group decision-making* (pp. 175-196). Beverly Hills, CA: Sage.

Putnam, L. L., & Jones, T. S. (1982). The role of communication in bargaining. *Human Communication Research, 8,* 262-280.

Putnam, L. L., & Wilson, C. E. (1982). Communicative strategies in organizational conflicts: Reliability and validity of a measurement scale. In M. Burgoon (Ed.), *Communication yearbook 6* (pp. 629-652). Beverly Hills, CA: Sage.

Pyke, D. L. (1970). A practical approach to Delphi. *Futures, 2,* 141.

Rahim, M. A. (1983). A measure of styles of handling interpersonal conflict. *Academy of Management Journal, 26,* 368-376.

Rawlinson, J. G. (1981). *Creative thinking and brainstorming.* New York: John Wiley.

Reagan, P., & Rohrbaugh, J. (1990). Group decision process effectiveness: A competing values approach. *Group & Organization Studies, 15,* 20-43.

Reamer, F. G. (1990). *Ethical dilemmas in social service* (2nd ed.). New York: Columbia University Press.

Reed, B. G., & Garvin, C. D. (1983). Group work with women/group work with men [Combined issue]. *Social Work With Groups, 6*(3/4).

Riggs, C. J. (1983). Dimensions of organizational conflict: A functional analysis of communication tactics. In R. N. Bostrom (Ed.), *Communication yearbook 7* (pp. 517-532). Beverly Hills, CA: Sage.

Robert, H. (1989). *Robert's rules of order.* New York: Berkeley Books.

Roby, T. B. (1952). The influence of subgroup relationships on the performance of group and subgroup tasks. *American Psychologist, 7,* 313-314.

Roethlisberger, E. J., & Dickson, W. J. (1939). *Management and the worker.* Cambridge, MA: Harvard University Press.

Rohrbaugh, J. (1981). Improving the quality of group judgment: Social judgment analysis and the nominal group technique. *Organizational Behavior and Human Performance, 28,* 272-288.

Rohrbaugh, J. (1988). Cognitive conflict task and small group processes. In B. Brehmer & C. R. B. Joyce (Eds.), *Human judgement: The SJT view* (pp. 199-226). Amsterdam: North-Holland.

Rose, S. R. (1989). Members leaving groups: Theoretical and practice considerations. *Small Group Behavior, 20,* 524-535.

Rothman, J. (1979). Three models of community organization practice, their mixing and phasing. In F. M. Cox, J. L. Erlich, J. Rothman, & J. E. Tropman (Eds.), *Strategies of community organization* (3rd ed., pp. 22-38). Itasca, IL: F. E. Peacock.

Rotter, G. S., & Portugal, S. M. (1969). Group and individual effects in problem solving. *Journal of Applied Psychology, 53,* 338-341.

Ruesch, J., & Bateson, G. (1951). *Communication: The social matrix of psychiatry.* New York: Norton.

Sachs, J. (1991). Action and reflection in work with a group of homeless people. *Social Work With Groups, 14,* 187-202.

Sage, P., Olmsted, D., & Atlesk, F. (1955). Predicting maintenance of membership in small groups. *Journal of Abnormal and Social Psychology, 51,* 308-331.

Sands, R. G., Stafford, J., & McClelland, M. (1990). "I beg to differ": Conflict in the interdisciplinary team. *Social Work in Health Care, 14,* 55-72.

Scheidel, T. M. (1986). Divergent and convergent thinking in group decision-making. In R. Y. Hirokawa & M. S. Poole (Eds.), *Communication and group decision-making* (pp. 113-132). Beverly Hills, CA: Sage.

Scheidel, T., & Crowell, L. (1979). *Discussing and deciding: A deskbook for group leaders and members.* New York: Macmillan.

Schweiger, D. M., Sandberg, W. R., & Ragan, J. W. (1986). Group approaches for improving strategic decision making: A comparative analysis of dialectical inquiry, devil's advocacy, and consensus. *Academy of Management Journal, 29,* 51-71.

Seaberg, J., & Gillespie, D. (1977). Goal attainment scaling: A critique. *Social Work Research and Abstracts, 13,* 4-9.

Sedek, G., Kofta, M., & Tyszka, T. (1993). Effects of uncontrollability on subsequent decision making: Testing the cognitive exhaustion hypothesis. *Journal of Personality and Social Psychology, 65,* 1270-1281.

Selinske, J. (1981). *A survey of the use and functioning of multidisciplinary teams in child protection services.* Washington, DC: National Professional Resource Center in Child Abuse and Neglect, American Public Welfare Association.

Shapiro, B. Z. (1991). Social action, the group and society. *Social Work With Groups, 14,* 4-21.

Shaver, P., & Buhrmester, D. (1984). Loneliness, sex-role orientation and group life: A social needs perspective. In P. B. Paulus (Ed.), *Basic group processes* (pp. 259-288). New York: Springer Verlag.

Shaw, M. E. (1976). *Group dynamics: The psychology of small group behavior* (2nd ed.). New York: McGraw-Hill.

Shaw, M. E. (1981). *Group dynamics: The psychology of small group behavior* (3rd ed.). New York: McGraw-Hill.

Shaw, M. E., & Shaw, L. M. (1962). Some effects of sociometric grouping upon learning in a second grade classroom. *Journal of Social Psychology, 57,* 453-458.

Shepherd, C. (1964). *Small groups.* San Francisco: Chandler.

Shulman, L. (1982). *Skills of supervision and staff management.* Itasca, IL: F. E. Peacock.

Simmel, G. (1950). *The sociology of George Simmel* (K. H. Wolff, Ed. & Trans.). Glencoe, IL: Free Press.

Siporin, M. (1986). Group work method and the inquiry. In P. H. Glasser & N. S. Mayadas (Eds.), *Group workers at work: Theory and practice in the eighties* (pp. 34-49). Totowa, NJ: Rowman & Littlefield.

Slater, P. E. (1955). Contrasting correlates of group size. *Sociometry, 21,* 129-139.

Smith, J. M. (1972). *Interviewing in market and social research.* London: Routledge & Kegan Paul.

Smith, P. (1978). Group work as a process of social influence. In N. McCaughan (Ed.), *Group work: Learning and practice* (pp. 36-57). London: Allen & Unwin.

Somers, M. L. (1976). Problem solving in small groups. In R. W. Roberts & H. Northen (Eds.), *Theories of social work with groups* (pp. 331-367). New York: Columbia University Press.

Sommer, R. (1969). *Personal space: The behavioral basis of design.* Englewood Cliffs, NJ: Prentice Hall.

Speroff, B., & Kerr, W. (1952). Steel mill "hot strip" accidents and interpersonal desirability values. *Journal of Clinical Psychology, 8,* 89-91.

Stahelski, A. J., & Tsukuda, R. A. (1990). Predictors of cooperation in health care teams. *Small Group Research, 21,* 220-233.

Stewart, D. W., & Shamdasani, P. M. (1990). *Focus groups: Theory and practice.* Newbury Park, CA: Sage.

Stouffer, S. (1949). *The American soldier, combat and its aftermath.* Princeton, NJ: Princeton University Press.

Strupp, H. H., & Hausman, H. J. (1953). Some correlates of group productivity. *American Psychologist, 7,* 443-444.

Swap, W. C., & Associates. (1984). *Group decision-making.* Beverly Hills, CA: Sage.

Taylor, D. W., Berry, P. C., & Block, C. H. (1958). Does group participation when using brainstorming facilitate or inhibit creative thinking? *Administrative Science Quarterly, 3,* 23-47.

Thalhofer, N. N. (1993). Intergroup differentiation and reduction of intergroup conflict. *Small Group Research, 24,* 28-43.

Thelen, H. (1954). *Dynamics of group work.* Chicago: University of Chicago Press.

Thomas, E., & Fink, C. (1963). Effects of group size. *Psychological Bulletin, 60,* 371-384.

Thomas, E. J. (1984). *Designing interventions for the helping professions.* Beverly Hills, CA: Sage.

Toseland, R. W., Ivanoff, A., & Rose, S. R. (1987). Treatment conferences: Task groups in action. *Social Work With Groups, 10,* 79-94.

Toseland, R. W., Palmer-Ganeles, G., & Chapman, D. (1986). Teamwork in psychiatric settings. *Social Work, 31,* 46-52.

Toseland, R. W., & Rivas, R. F. (1984). *An introduction to group work practice.* New York: Macmillan.

Toseland, R. W., & Rivas, R. F. (1994). *An introduction to group work practice* (2nd ed.). New York: Macmillan.

Toseland, R. W., Rivas, R. F., & Chapman, D. (1984). An evaluation of decision-making methods in task groups. *Social Work, 29,* 339-346.

Trecker, H. B. (1948). *Social group work: Principles and practice.* New York: Association Press.

Trecker, H. B. (1955). *Group worker: Foundation and frontiers.* New York: Whiteside.

Trecker, H. B. (1980). Administration as a group process: Philosophy and concepts. In A. S. Alissi (Ed.), *Perspectives on social group work practice* (pp. 332-339). New York: Free Press.

Tropman, J. E., & Morningstar, G. (1985). *Meetings: How to make them work for you.* New York: Macmillan.

Uhl, N. (1971). *Encouraging convergence of opinions through the use of the Delphi technique in the process of identifying institutional goals.* Princeton, NJ: Educational Testing Service.

Van Gundy, A. B. (1987). *Creative problem solving: A guide for trainers and management.* New York: Quorem.

Van Gundy, A. B. (1988). *Techniques of structured problem-solving* (2nd ed.). New York: Van Nostrand Reinhold.

Van Zelst, R. H. (1952a). Sociometrically selected work teams increase production. *Personnel Psychology, 5,* 175-186.

Van Zelst, R. H. (1952b). Validation of a sociometric regrouping procedure. *Journal of Abnormal and Social Psychology, 47,* 299-301.

Vinter, R. D. (1985). Program activities: An analysis of their effects on participant behavior. In M. Sundel, P. Glasser, R. Sarri, & R. Vinter (Eds.), *Individual change through small groups* (2nd ed., pp. 226-236). New York: Free Press.

Vroom, V. H., & Yetton, P. W. (1973). *Leadership and decision-making.* Pittsburgh: University of Pittsburgh Press.

Wagner, W. G. (1987). Child sexual abuse: A multidisciplinary approach to case management. *Journal of Counseling and Development, 65,* 435-439.

Waldinger, R. J. (1990). *Psychiatry for medical students* (2nd ed.). Washington, DC: American Psychiatric Press.

Wall, V. D., Jr., & Nolan, L. L. (1986). Perceptions of inequity, satisfaction, and conflict in task-oriented groups. *Human Relations, 19,* 1033-1052.

Warner, W. L., Meeker, M., & Eells, K. (1949). *Social class in America.* Chicago: Social Science Research Associates.

Watt, J. W. (1985). Protective service teams: The social worker as liaison. *Health and Social Work, 10,* 191-197.

Weaver, T. W. (1971). The Delphi forecasting method. *Phi Delta Kappan, 52,* 267-271.

Webster's Tenth New Collegiate Dictionary. (1992). Springfield, MA: Merriam-Webster.

Weingart, L. R., & Weldon, E. (1991). Processes that mediate the relationship between group goal and group member performance. *Human Performance, 4,* 33-54.

Weiss, C. H. (1972). *Evaluation research: Methods of assessing program effectiveness.* Englewood Cliffs, NJ: Prentice Hall.

Wells, W. D. (1974). Group interviewing. In R. Ferber (Ed.), *Handbook of marketing research* (pp. 133-146). New York: McGraw-Hill.

Williams, J. B., & Spitzer, R. L. (1984). *Psychotherapy research: Where are we and where should we go?* New York: Guilford.

Williams, K. (1981, May). *The effects of group cohesion on social loafing.* Paper presented at the annual meeting of the Midwestern Psychological Association, Detroit, MI.

Wilson, G. (1976). From practice to theory: A personalized history. In R. W. Roberts &
    H. Northen (Eds.), *Theories of social work with groups* (pp. 1-44). New York: Columbia
    University Press.

Wilson, G., & Ryland, G. (1949). *Social group work practice.* Cambridge, MA: Riverside.

Zander, A. (1982). *Making groups effective.* San Francisco: Jossey-Bass.

Zastrow, C. (1985). *Social work with groups.* Chicago: Nelson-Hall.

Zimet, C. N., & Schneider, C. (1969). Effects of group size on interaction in small groups.
    Journal of Social Psychology, 77, 177-187.

INDEX

ABOUT THE AUTHORS

Marian Fatout is Associate Professor and Chair of the Children and Families Concentration at the Louisiana State University School of Social Work. She received her M.S.W. and D.S.W. from the University of Southern California. She has held professional positions in health, mental health, and child and family welfare settings that involved work with task groups. Her research interests and publications pertain to the structures, processes, and uses of groups. She has been a member of the Association for the Advancement of Social Work with Groups since its inception.

Steven R. Rose is Associate Professor and Chair of the Mental Health Concentration at the Louisiana State University School of Social Work. He received his M.S.W. from Washington University (St. Louis) and his PH.D. from the University of Wisconsin—Madison. He has held faculty positions at the Hebrew University of Jerusalem and the University of Vermont. He has held professional positions in mental health, children and families, and education and school settings that involved work with task groups. His research and publication area is small group processes and interventions.